Down Detour Road

Down Detour Road

An Architect in Search of Practice

Eric J. Cesal

The MIT Press
Cambridge, Massachusetts
London, England

For information about special quantity discounts, please email special_sales@ mitpress.mit.edu

This book was set in Stone serif and Stone sans by Graphic Composition, Inc. Printed and bound in the United States of America.

Library of Congress Cataloging-in-Publication Data

Cesal, Eric J., 1977–
Down detour road : an architect in search of practice / Eric J. Cesal.
  p. cm.
Includes bibliographical references and index.
ISBN 978-0-262-01461-8 (pbk. : alk. paper) 1. Architectural practice. I. Title.
II. Title: Architect in search of practice.
 NA1995.C42 2010
 720.23—dc22

                                    2010002551

10 9 8 7 6 5 4 3

Contents

Acknowledgments

An extended set of acknowledgments is necessary. This text was written quite spontaneously, during a period of unemployment, as both chronicle and catharsis. I would therefore like to thank not only those who participated in the actual editing and writing, but those who formed a backdrop of support in what was otherwise a trying time.

I will begin by thanking my mother Gloria, my father Lon, and my stepmother Rose, who have been encouraging my architecture since it was made from Legos, and my writing since it was in crayon. Their steadiness during a time of uncertainty made me realize just how much they'd always been there. They helped in all the ways that parents do, and I'm sure that the full scope of their contribution will elude me, at least until I have my own children.

The support of my sister Chiara Vega was equally strong and perhaps even more remarkable, considering she didn't agree with the book's direction—she had hoped that it might be a bit less wonkish and more mass-market. As she always has, she threw her support behind me, even when she couldn't figure out what I was doing with my life.

I would also like to thank several former teachers who graciously listened over the years while the ideas in this book were taking shape. While there have been many teachers throughout my career without whom I couldn't have assembled these thoughts, the ones that participated most directly were Peter MacKeith, Dr. Paula Lupkin, and Bruce Lindsey, AIA, all of whom not only served as critical sounding boards during the writing but went out of their way to send periodic odd jobs my way, thus dampening the sting of unemployment.

Special thanks are also due to my editor Roger Conover, as well as Susan Clark, Matthew Abbate, Yasuyo Iguchi, and the whole staff at the MIT Press, for their invaluable assistance in bringing this book to fruition. As much as for their guidance, I should thank them for their patience in dealing with the anxieties of a first-time author.

A close circle of friends volunteered to be early reviewers of the manuscript. I owe a special thanks to Cristina Greavu, Andrew Malick, and Michael Heller for their generous and detailed reviews. Their insight kept me honest and their company kept me smiling.

My attorney, Wendi Chapman, Esq., in addition to being a font of legal advice, is a constant source of optimism and seemingly has always known when I needed prodding.

Thanks to Fidel Ortega, AIA, Patrick Williams, AIA, and Jate Yonkos, not only for mentoring me during my early years but for keeping me tethered to my professional roots while I was meandering through academia. Their candid insights and perspective were invaluable.

To Dr. Andrew Tassler and Bob Rich, who have been with me through the long haul and whose friendship and humor have never wavered. It is no exaggeration to say that they marshaled my sanity at all the right times, and provided the support I needed to complete this book.

Finally, to my partner Cristina Garmendia, who knew that this book was worth writing, worth publishing, and worth reading, even before I started it. Her love and support were certainly an act of pure, unconditional faith.

1 | Introduction: Reflections from Detour Road

My departure from grad school must have looked like one of those baby birds trying to fly out of the nest before it was ready. Not that I wasn't ready, but I imagine the motions appeared similar. Some tepid eyes, some panicked flapping, a slow helical descent. A damp thud. It was one of those things that happened before I realized it was happening, like the first time I had sex or the first time I had my heart broken.

Life threw me a few more curveballs than usual in that last week, and amid the spinning and the flapping I tried to remember how the noodle had been simmering five years prior, when I entered graduate school optimistically.

Meditating on life and architectural philosophy as I made my exit from the academy was like dancing when you're dead drunk. I was impressed with myself at the time, but I hope no one videotaped it and I probably owe someone an apology. The final hours of my departure were done in the dark, and sheets of freezing rain slicked the roads to a glare and the trees to a knotty black. The day after Final Review, I moved my belongings into storage, on what turned out to be the coldest day of that particular winter. There was much I didn't get done, but I had no time to mourn, or pause, or reflect. It was three days to Christmas—I got in the car and started moving.

Long-distance drives are great for thinking, or at least thinking you're thinking. The long stretch of highway and shifting red spots turn cheeky observations into deep philosophical insights. They perhaps set the stage for what was to come.

I crash-landed at my father's house in rural Maryland, between Washington, D.C. and the Atlantic. He had moved out there after my sister and I left for college in order to start a tree nursery—his retirement project. I first found Detour Road that day.

Coming off Final Review, naps come over you like a sneeze—spontaneous and irresistible. That day I sank into a soft bed and a broad pillow and let my body try and piece back together what architecture school had done its best to break down. An indeterminate time later I awoke and stumbled out the door, groggy but finally taking pause, and found beauty.

My father lives in the way, way out. He has one visible neighbor, and that neighbor has one visible building. A greenhouse of corrugated plastic. The sun was setting over my left shoulder and its purple and pink rays were getting caught in the corrugations of the plastic. Every panel captured the light differently. The strong wind must have been oil-canning the panels, because the surface of the building shimmered organically, like bright rocks under moving water. The building was alive by pure accident.

Perhaps it was just post-finals delirium, but I found myself entranced by this simple greenhouse. I had spent the better part of the last ten years seeking out architecture. Trying to understand it, to define it, to make it, and in some way to capture it in chipboard and styrene. Driving back across the country, I was possessed by the thought that I had failed in those efforts. Not

Figure 1.1
Architecture?

only could I not find architecture in what I was doing, I couldn't find architecture in what anyone else was doing. I had so many working definitions of the word that I couldn't decide for myself whether any particular thing was architecture or not. The word had ceased to mean anything to me.

I paused at the stoop and thought this could be the basis of a good book. The story of a young man who went deep into the bowels of the academy in order to understand architecture and found it had been on his doorstep all along. This had an air of hokeyness about it, but it had been a tough couple of days and I was feeling sentimental about the warm confines of the studio that had unceremoniously discharged me upon the world. The family piled into the car to head out to dinner—a celebration of my supposed triumph (finishing grad school, not discovering architecture). As we were sailing through the back highways of the Eastern Shore of Maryland, I came across more "architecture": a road called Detour Road. My mind wanted to stop and admire this clever road sign, but my stomach, perhaps understanding that it was about to get its first complete meal in over a month, commanded silence. So we drove on. I returned by foot the next day, admiring this little contradiction in the winter's setting sun. Walking seemed appropriate, because I didn't particularly have anything else to do. I was confronting, for the first time in a decade, the question of how to fill up my day.

Another question was nagging me more. I couldn't figure out whether I was attracted to the street sign out of sentimentality, or whether it really was pregnant with the meaning I thought was there. For all the years that I had spent trying to find meaning and purpose in my architecture—in any architecture—this accidental piece of signage had achieved what I had not. Meaning perspired off the sign while I sat on the side of the road,

Figure 1.2
Harmony not included.

on the bare earth, waiting for the light to get just right. The sign was my whole life. It was a detour that somehow became a road. I meditated on the fact that detours aren't something you choose to take; you take detours when the road that you want to take has been closed, washed out, bombed through, or is otherwise unavailable.

Detours are longer and less direct, and yet often show us parts of the place that we otherwise never would have visited. They expand our experience and our knowledge, even when we would rather have taken our regular road. My life had, up to that point, been a series of accidents and mistakes that somehow found purpose and validation. For all the things I had intended my life to be, for all the things I thought I would be doing at 31, I was sitting in the dirt, on the side of an empty, unlit road, jobless, homeless, cold and hungry, lusting after a street sign. And yet contained within this oxymoron was the whole story. My life, and my architecture, were no longer a detour. They had become a road. I had boots (for walking), a laptop (for writing), a mind (for thinking), hands (for crafting), and people who cared about me (for everything else). That's all an architect really needs, I thought. I shrugged off the cold, walked home, and started writing.

An editor once told me that I shouldn't ever try to write a book on something unless I was the world's expert on it. When I got to a point where there wasn't a single other person on Earth who knew my subject matter better than I did, the book would essentially write itself. Having just waded into the worst economic crisis in a generation, I didn't particularly feel like an expert on anything. Merriam-Webster defines an expert as "one with the special skill or knowledge representing mastery of a particular subject," and my skills and knowledge were much more of the general kind.

A few days prior to my encounter with Detour Road I had finished the final jury for my master's in architecture—my third master's degree in four years. My "special skill" seemed to be acquiring advanced degrees. Prior to that I had worked as an intern architect for five years or so, and I knew that the professional world that I was entering was much changed from the one I had left behind. I wandered home after the jury contemplating the fact that for the first time in my adult life I was neither enrolled nor employed. I was ronin. The economic crisis of 2008–? was just beginning to bite down on St. Louis and the evidence was mounting, even on the three-block walk from the school of architecture to my apartment. Off to my left, a construction project stood idle. The coffee shop I usually passed by seemed to have too many people in it. And at school, my classmates were filtering out, physically and psychologically, into a world that seemed unenthusiastic about their arrival.

I had previously gotten a master of business administration as well, and although no expert, I knew enough about the worlds of finance and economics to know that this was going to be more than an ordinary recession. I also knew that it would be a few months before the general consciousness caught up to that reality and the panic of the talking heads became the panic of the masses. Finance people had been warily watching this bubble grow for several years, and knew that its bursting would destroy many of our notions about our economy and society. It would be different from the previous bubbles.

My ruminations on the economic crisis were complicated by the fact that it had no name. We had already had a "Great Depression," and Japan had its "Lost Decade." I knew that ten years from now our current crisis would have a name. It would be something somber yet articulate. I didn't have time for the wonks to think one up, so I gave it my own: the Great Wake. I leave the term open to interpretation.

The basis of the Great Wake, and why it differs from previous recessions, are conceptually easy to understand. Any free economy will suffer boom and bust cycles. We've gotten better at controlling their volatility, but at some level they're always going to happen. A boom occurs around some event: a discovery, a technology, a sociological transformation. Gold is discovered in California. The personal computer is invented. A war ends. It could be any number of things. At the very beginning, there will be a limited number of visionaries and daredevils who jump on the wagon before anyone else knows what's going on. These are the early adopters—the people who invested in Microsoft in 1981. As the boom expands, the adventurousness of the few is validated; the general public begins to see that these few were right: there *is* gold in California, and the Internet *is* actually quite useful. More people become interested.

As more and more people become interested, the price of buying into the prosperity is driven up. At the height of the boom, there is so much hysteria from so many that the price is *inflated*. That is, the price exceeds what the thing is actually worth in an alternate, nonhysterical world. The most recent and readily understood example of this occurred during the IT nineties, when seemingly rational people would buy stock in emerging companies that had no products, no offices, and no plan. And they would pay handsomely for it.

At some point, the market catches up to the idea that prices have been overshot—it corrects. In the tail end of the boom, prices fall downward until that inflated selling price comes back into line with reality.

The interesting thing is that in almost all instances, they don't fall back to zero. However severe the bust is, we are left with something significant. After all, it had to be something very powerful to get the boom started in the first place. After the 1849 Gold Rush, many were disappointed to find out that they weren't going to strike it rich, but we had *California*. Many of us still remember taking a bath when the IT bubble burst, but at the end of the day the boom gave us instantaneous global communication. As a society, as a culture, we had progressed and gained significantly.

What is different about our current recession, and the reason economists frequently compare it to the Great Depression or the Dutch Tulip Craze, is that there is no underlying value in the commodities at stake. The line has fallen back to zero. A mortgage-backed security is exactly what it sounds like—a security backed by a mortgage. A mortgage is just a promise to pay a certain amount of money. Once the person has decided to break that promise, the mortgage and the security are *literally* only worth the paper that they're printed on. Sure, you could get someone else to buy it, but who would pay $400,000 for a piece of paper that only really legally entitles them to a $200,000 house?

New terms came into the public consciousness in late 2008: hedging, insurance, credit default swaps—all of which are, for our purposes here, the same thing. They are promises to pay. Once that promise is violated, all that's left is a bunch of paper. There is no land, no product, no patent.

It is for this reason that economists, pundits, and politicians regard the Great Wake so differently, and for this reason the ensuing recovery will not look like the recovery from the early eighties, or early nineties, or the 2001 recession. We will restructure how and why we buy things—not just put off purchases until the mist clears.

This is especially relevant for architects and other design professionals, because the subject of our work is expensive. Buying a house is the most expensive personal decision most of us will ever make. Buying a building is similarly serious for an organization or government. These decisions are rarely made on a whim or paid for with cash. Buildings are bought with credit. Society's need for buildings is not going to disappear, but we are going to fundamentally reimagine how and why we buy them. As architects, we must also rethink our methods to respond to this new reality, and not just wait for the work to pick up again.

The implications were unfolding across the news and in my employment prospects. I raised an eyebrow when Lehman Brothers went under. But I was in the thesis semester of my master's in architecture, and couldn't be bothered to think too much about it. As the economy went from sputtering to outright collapse, I began to understand the Great Wake as a cultural event, not just a financial one. We would likely never have another Great Depression—but the Great Wake would reshape us, as the Great Depression had. It would rework our values and our leanings and our politics. It might even change our architecture. This crisis stemmed from the fact that the richest country in the world now had a wealth that was not derived from the value of its work or its products. Much of our "wealth" was, for lack of a better word, imaginary. It was the result of financial, legal, or political tautologies. Where once we created value through work, innovation, and industry, now, we create wealth through imagination and policy. We had, as a nation, built a castle on the sand.

Operating between the worlds of finance and design, I wondered how this castle would crumble. It seems logical that our nation will move back to a more centrist, disciplined lifestyle. It will expect more accountability out of its politicians. In the broadest terms, we will put more faith in what we can see, and touch, and rely on. Rather than pouring our life savings into speculative, exploding real estate markets, or mysterious financial vehicles like the credit-swap derivative, Americans might rediscover the simple merits of a savings account. Instead of using the power of unlimited credit to finance riskier and riskier ventures, Americans might return to the simple concept of value.

In their built environment, they might expect better results, and they are unlikely to confuse "grandiose" with "good," as the last generation has. Rather than looking at their homes as a way to make some money, they might again look upon them as a way to make some security. And they would be less inclined to tolerate disinvestment in their built spaces merely to procure a small, short-term tax break. They may awaken to the fact that they have traded their children's future for a brief, small party.

However we, as a nation, emerge from this crisis, we know that we will be changed. Architecture, too, must change, as the professional topography will be different. Architects always have to do things a bit differently during lean times. But aside from the usual "lay off 20 percent of the staff and skimp on test plots" mentality that seems to grip architects in a recession, we must be aware of the fact that we are in the midst of a cultural and psychological watershed. As guardians and champions of culture, and as stewards of the built environment, we must consider how this will change us—how it *must* change us.

I kept a nervous finger on these ideas throughout my thesis semester. They'd occasionally bounce into my head like a dirty thought in church. But as any architect knows, thesis semester is not a time for abstract brooding, at least not on matters unrelated to one's thesis. Besides, I had other problems. My lease was running out. Without a job, I'd be unable to sign a new one. I had some dental work that was falling apart—and I had been expectantly waiting for employment to bless me with dental insurance so that I could get it taken care of. With the prospect of being jobless, homeless, *and* toothless, I had to confront the idea that my design skills were not worth anything. Of course they were of value to me, and I'm sure that the ones who taught me those skills considered such teaching valuable. I know that I paid a lot for them. But in confronting the gruesome absence of employment, I had to wonder what their value was.

Around the same time, a report from the U.K. Office for National Statistics detailed the increase in unemployment for 354 different professions from February 2008 to February 2009. Overall, the average increase in unemployment claims was 98 percent—that is, for every 100 people unemployed in 2008, there were now 198 unemployed. It seemed consistent with the general reports of a rough doubling of the unemployment rate. Coming as no surprise to my architect colleagues, architects topped the list. There had been nearly an eightfold increase in the number of unemployed architects in just the prior year. As outrageous as this seemed, it seemed to wash over every colleague I showed it to. It was greeted with a shrug: "Yeah, I guess it sucks to be an architect." More interesting to me than the fact that architects were at the top was the fact that they were so far away from the average. No other profession was even close. Brokers and financial managers, the ones who seemingly had caused the economic crisis, were only suffering unemployment at rates 1½ times greater than before. Even professions that also operated on the built environment, like carpenters and civil engineers, had only increased their unemployment around 2½ times over the prior year.

Why were architects at an eightfold increase? What could explain architecture's incredible standing among 354 surveyed professions? I wondered aloud to anyone who would listen. The response from nonarchitects was usually skepticism. "Dead last, really?" they would ask, somehow suspicious that I was inflating numbers to console myself over my own employment prospects. Worse yet, the response from the architects I knew was typically muted. Times are tough. Things will come back. The stimulus plan will save us. The older architects remembered prior recessions and opined that we will survive this one, too.

These exchanges were for me a window into an unsettling aspect of architectural professional culture. We seem to wear these tough times almost as a badge of honor—they reveal how much we love our craft. We question whether we will have the mettle to survive the tough times—but we don't seem to discuss why things are so tough in the first place.

Given the crisis, I felt things should be *less* tough. I felt my design skills should be more valuable than ever. The financial crisis had been about our built environment—about mortgage-backed securities. The health care crisis is also about architecture, inasmuch as we spend more on hospitals in this country than we do on doctors. Housing—the formaldehyde-free kind—is our first line of defense in guarding our nation's health. The construction industry is one of our country's largest employers, making it a major part of our unemployment crisis. And climate change is also an architectural problem, inasmuch as the bulk of our emissions and landfill waste comes from buildings. As the crisis bubbled and the country reoriented, it seemed one should find architects in the center of the storm. Whatever part architects played in the formation of the day's problems, it seemed they should have an intelligent role in their resolution. A designer's ability to frame problems, to think synthetically, to rapidly oscillate between massive scales and tiny ones seemed like it would be useful. In a time of great uncertainty and change, a designer's services would be in demand.

It was clearly not the case, however. Someone forgot to tell the job market, and my inbox was empty. No one was calling any architects, asking for their opinion on how to address the nation's problems. There was no cabinet-level position on architecture. I resisted the temptation to externalize the blame to those outside the profession—it was architects who had positioned themselves in the public's eye in a way that left them detached from these sorts of grimy problems. The most famous architects of the past generation made their image behind megastructures: the museum, the corporate tower, the library, the stadium. Obviously, other work was also being done, but on the cover of *Time* magazine architects fill a narrow mold. Whatever it was, there was one thing it was not: the architect wasn't someone you called during an economic crisis.

So my phone wasn't ringing. One of two things had to be true:

1. I had no valuable skills.
2. I had skills, but the world had yet to be convinced of their value.

I wondered if, at some point, the "special skill" that Merriam-Webster described would reveal itself, like a fire extinguisher that only really finds itself useful if there's a fire. The rest of the time it's just taking up space. There was just no fire, presently, and there wasn't anything wrong, in particular, with me or that which I had spent the last four years studying. I tossed the metaphor around in my head while packing up the contents of my apartment for my move to nowhere. In rooting through my kitchen (which had gotten little use over my graduate years, as most of my sustenance came through studio vending machine goodies), I found, in an act of providence, a fire extinguisher. Buried in a cupboard, behind some mostly empty bottles of liquor and some mostly full cleaning supplies, was a petite fire extinguisher that I had bought when I moved in. I suddenly remembered buying it as I settled in and thinking myself quite a practical fellow—I was preparing for disaster! I was thinking progressively. And if there ever were a fire, I could deal with it swiftly and confidently, saving my two cats from a fiery demise!

The trouble with my plan, obviously, was that over the years I had forgotten all about the fire extinguisher. If there had been a fire at any point during my graduate years, you would have found me out on the street, a cat under each arm, cursing myself for not having had the foresight to buy a fire extinguisher. The fire marshal would emerge from the smoldering ruin of my building with a mangled, unused fire extinguisher and ask, "Why didn't you just use this?"

As I tried to finish off my reserves of alcohol and cleaning supplies, I wondered aloud how much our profession held in common with my lost fire extinguisher. Something whose value is conceptually easy to understand, but which goes unused and unappreciated because people do not know it's there. Certainly, our society is aware that architecture exists as a profession, and equally aware that these professionals get paid something for their efforts. But every architect has occasionally had the suspicion that the public at large understands very little about what we do. That the task of *design* is even more misunderstood. Our clients varyingly understand us as artists, or project managers, or decipherers of code, or producers of blueprints, or guardians of a stamp, or blowhards, etc. Most architects would argue vehemently that "design" lies at the heart of what we do, but you will get as many definitions for that word as there are architects. It is also certain that if we cannot agree on a definition of "design," our clients aren't rushing to find one either.

This vagueness of what it means to be an architect assaulted me as I entered the job market. I started throwing my resume onto online job services like www.monster.com, a process that involves setting up "alerts" that troll listed job offerings to locate listings containing characteristics or keywords that you specify. What I noticed very quickly is that most of the job offerings for "architect" involved nothing of the kind. There were listings for "database architect" and "digital security architect" and my favorite: "solutions architect." The word "architect" had become so washed out that "solutions" had to be attached to it, to distinguish it from those architects that just made problems, I supposed. At any rate, there were no jobs for "architect" as I understood that term. It occurred to me that over the last generation, while a bunch of smart people anguished over the distinction between "architect" and "designer" and "intern architect" or "interior architect," *someone stole our damn name.*

A guy who fixes cars is a mechanic, not an "automotive doctor." And the guy who dry-cleaned my suits (back when I owned some) never referred to himself as a "professor of cleaning." But somehow, different professions seem to have grown comfortable appropriating the word "architect." While we struggled to understand what that word should mean to us, we came to ignore the fact that it no longer means anything to them.

There are architects among us who have prospered in this decay. As the profession confronted the question of what it means to be an architect in a postmodernist world, many took advantage of the ambivalence to make claims that heretofore would have seemed outrageous. Architecture should follow *no* organizing set of principles. Architecture shouldn't be rooted in history or urbanity or cities or even clients; it must be "distanced from any external value system."[1] This movement was canonized in 1988, in an exhibition organized by Philip Johnson and Mark Wigley that included many of the most famous names in contemporary architecture, among them Frank Gehry, Daniel Libeskind, Rem Koolhaas, Peter Eisenman, Zaha Hadid.

Ironically, these architects go to great lengths to disassociate themselves from the term that would bind them all:

deconstruction. And yet the term has gained considerable currency among architects to describe this panoply of architectural ideas. The term emerged not to capture a unifying idea, but to describe the absence of one. As we debated the pros and cons of each of these possibilities, the ambivalence became institutionalized. How much fun it was to revel in the possibilities—to debate and to write and to teach and to froth about what architecture could or couldn't be! After living under the rigidity of modernism for the better part of the century, new movements would give architects room to run.

But in the ambivalence, another change transpired. With no clear definition emanating from our profession, the outside world had no sharp picture of what an architect should or could do.

The pictures are, if not consistent, at least mostly positive. An oft-traded article among architects concerns the results of a survey conducted by the London dating agency Drawing Down the Moon. In this survey, architecture is found to be "the sexiest male profession," at least according to the ladies of London. Architects were recorded as "balanced and rounded individuals who combine a creative approach with a caring, thoughtful disposition." It was unclear whether any of the respondents had ever had to date an architect, and while it would be interesting to see such a parsing of the data, the overall point remains clear: architects ranked higher than stockbrokers or doctors in their overall sexiness.

This esteem and sexiness are used for humorous con on screen. George Costanza in the show *Seinfeld* famously impersonated an architect for a variety of reasons. In *There's Something about Mary,* both Lee Evans's and Matt Dillon's characters impersonate architects in order to gain the affections of the film's title character, played by Cameron Diaz. There is, at least to Mary, also something sexy (and trustworthy) about being an architect.

The flip side to this is expressed in an open letter to architects by Annie Choi, originally published in the magazine *Pidgin*. Choi bemoans her architect friends' constant whining about how little they sleep, how much they work, how little they make, but more importantly she questions their overall professional usefulness:

> I believe that architecture falls somewhere between toenail fungus and invasive colonoscopy in the list of things that interest me.

And

> I have a friend who is a doctor. He gives me drugs. I enjoy them. I have a friend who is a lawyer. He helped me sue my landlord. My architect friends have given me nothing. . . . One architect friend figured out that my apartment was one hundred and eighty-seven square feet. That was nice. Thanks for that.[2]

The "Dear Architects" letter is only three pages long, but has probably been traded among every architecture student in the country. For many of the students I know, it marked the first encounter with the fear that people don't think too highly of us.

It explains, I think, why the only "architect" jobs on www .monster.com are for IT professionals. Generally, people don't have a clear idea of what we do, so the name itself is up for grabs. And how could they be expected to know what we do when one architect defines architecture as a space organization activity and another defines it as a sculpting of built shapes, or a professional service, and no common set of beliefs, skills, or principles holds us together? People are free to make up their own definitions.

As Choi observes, most of us have occasion to interact with a doctor on a regular basis. Most of us will, from time to time, require the services of a lawyer. Even if we don't, the worlds of medicine and law are presented to us in a seemingly endless parade of prime-time dramas and comedies. There are shows about cops, detectives, ad executives, forensic examiners, and even one about a UPS delivery guy. Architects watch these shows wistfully, bemoaning the fact that there are no accompanying shows about architects. Therefore, architects enjoy a mysterious air—a mixed blessing, as we will see.

It is notable that architects appear occasionally in movies— although the movies are rarely about them *as* architects. Consider Wesley Snipes in *Jungle Fever*, or Henry Fonda in *12 Angry Men*. The architect is portrayed as someone handsome, professional, and well-spoken. The only movies I have seen where architects are portrayed heroically are *The Towering Inferno* and *Death Wish*, and in neither case is the architect heroic with his architecture. In *The Towering Inferno*, the architecture is, in some respects, the villain; the movie ends with Paul Newman's "hero" architect admitting his hubris before the more rational and responsible fire chief. In *Death Wish*, Charles Bronson's idealistic architect gives up on architecture as a means of creating a better world, and discovers that shooting criminals is much more expedient and satisfying. Whatever dramas transpire, the action is never about the drama of *being* an architect and doesn't offer insight into what we do.

So it shouldn't come as any surprise that our name has been co-opted. But how to get it back? How can we represent to the world who we are and what we do when we can't agree ourselves?

The path of the medical profession can tell us a lot. In the same way that the word "architect" has become diluted, the word "doctor" meant a variety of things, once upon a time. Apart from our modern divisions between medical doctors and PhDs, there is little confusion about what doctors do. In either context, the word "doctor" is taken to mean an expert. We can reliably assume that someone with the title of "doctor" is someone who is well educated, well trained, and ethical. It wasn't always the case.

At one point, the government lacked the regulatory initiative or structure to police all the people who were running the countryside calling themselves "doctor." Anecdotally, becoming a doctor seemed to have been quite easy. You mixed a bunch of ingredients together in your bathtub, bottled it, got yourself a barker and a stagecoach and hit the road. There was little chance of such charlatans being arrested or prosecuted, though they did occasionally run the risk of being strung up by dissatisfied townsfolk. These snake oil salesmen prospered, so we must assume that at least some segment of the population was impressed. Many others could also address your medical issues. Barbers, surgeons, leech-wielders, and shamans were all competing in the same market. As described by Roy Porter:

> Life was also hard for many a "horse and buggy" doctor in the American Midwest; in rural Russia, the Australian outback and wherever else conditions were raw, patients formed a floating, feckless, hard-bitten population, and passing irregulars and medicine-show hucksters spelt rivalry.[3]

As early as the seventeenth century, *science* started to infect medicine, and radical ideas like "germs" started to work their way into practice. And yet it wasn't until the nineteenth century that the American Medical Association was formed, and the Food and Drug Administration wasn't formed until the break of the twentieth.

This lag meant that for two centuries, doctors who were highly educated and trained in scientific methods had to compete in an open market with all manner of clowns and charlatans. At some point, these learned men came to understand that they could not allow these other professions to prosper. They had two main reasons for such a stance: one ethical and one professional.

The ethical aspect is more or less obvious. Doctors—real ones—had an inkling of how damaging and fraudulent some of their competitors' activities were. They were aware that many snake oil salesmen weren't just selling bathtub Shirley Temples, but actual poisons. They could also prove, through scientific methods, that bloodletters and snake charmers were performing no service at all, and therefore had a huge informational advantage over the general public, which could only rely on anecdotal evidence and superstition.

Professionally, real doctors must have recognized that, on a market basis, they couldn't compete. They had to invest an enormous amount of time, money, and energy in their training. Their methods were probably consequently expensive. And a patient who could not distinguish between real medicine and quackery would have no reason to front the additional capital required to pay the doctor's fees. If a snake oil salesman can ply his trade for virtually nothing, than he can charge next to nothing. And if there is nothing to distinguish what he does from the expensive medicine that one might receive from a real doctor, why bother? Porter ascribes the rise of the modern medical profession to exactly this type of competition:

> And it was for these reasons—career insecurities—that reformers like Thomas Wakley (1795–1862), founder of the *Lancet* (1823), battled to raise medicine into a respected profession, with structured, regulated entry and lofty ethical ideals.[4]

Surely the medical profession realized, from an ethical standpoint, that quackery needed to be rooted out. But it was the professional need that probably galvanized doctors to action—the recognition that as long as quacks were allowed to do what they did, it would never be profitable for doctors to do what they do.

There are obvious differences between medicine and architecture, and no analogy is perfect. But as I confronted the most gruesome employment picture in a generation, my insecurities weren't entirely personal. They had more to do with my profession. I have been blessed to spend both my professional years and my academic years in the company of some extremely talented architects, and I could not wrap my brain around the fact that so many of them were unemployed. It wasn't me, or them. It was "the profession." It was a comfortable parsing, one that was necessary to get me psychologically through the first few months of unemployment and allowed me to start writing. If "the profession" was at fault, it raised a number of questions. Rather than understanding myself as a professional operating in a profession, or an artist operating in a culture, I began to think of architecture itself operating as a corporation in a market. The market was the built environment. Architecture (capital A) was a player—competing against other players (developers, mass homebuilders, etc.). Me, the profession, the fire extinguisher: we all had to be better about describing and advocating our value within this arena.

The first step in understanding our value is the uncomfortable embrace of the truth that what architects aspire to do and what they're capable of doing can be very different things. Every young architect begins his or her journey with some dream of acting on the built environment: a dream of being a shaper. The dream is not just about shaping steel and glass, but of shaping culture, experience, history, urbanity.

At some point in the journey, the architect comes to understand that the heroic image he or she has harbored is only a myth. An architect wields little control over the built environment. His or her choices are generally narrow and forced. Exceptions occur, of course. An architect may stumble into a measure of control by winning a very public design competition, although even then the architect's design is given as much authority as the competition organizers allow, and no more. A faithfully executed competition design entry may only mean that the powerless architect managed to curry the favor of some powerful people. Another exception may occur when an architect achieves such commanding brand power that powerful clients seek him or her out. Only then, again through the power of the clients as much as the power of the design, does the world of possibilities open up. We have come to define success in such ways: the success of those who, by design talent, or connections, or plain moxie, tap and exploit that narrow vein of possibility.

The success of these few, however, can sometimes retard the success of our profession. It does so when the activities of these few obfuscate the meaning of the word "architect" or otherwise diminish what is expected of the profession as a whole. When the same act of design can bring all the internal rewards of the profession yet at the same time turn the world away from architecture, we have become aimless. This aimlessness feeds a world that doesn't know and doesn't care about architecture. The current apathy toward architecture—that is, the extent to which most people don't care or don't know how much their environment is designed, or how well it is designed—results directly from the mechanics of success within our own profession.

Is reform possible? Medical history suggests yes. Different professions reinvent themselves constantly. Freud once speculated that cocaine could be used to cure morphine addiction. If medicine can get over *that*, then architecture can get over whatever mistakes we've made.

Architectural history, however, suggests maybe. Architectural history is replete with calls for reform, most of them centered on the same question: "What should an architect be?" The question has seemingly been around as long as the profession itself. Beginning in the Renaissance, the architect seemed to arise naturally out of other professions: the master mason, the sculptor, or the painter. Whoever took that title never formally trained for it and was not licensed for it. In nineteenth-century England, the profession seems to have attached great weight to distancing itself from those trades where it found its origins. The artistic and cultural functions of architecture took on special significance, because it was there that the architect could, on a market basis, distinguish himself from the builder or mason, who were typically illiterate and uneducated in the formal sense. In the following century, the architect was recast as a social engineer and technocrat—probably owing to the growing importance of industry and technology in everyday experience. We entered a world where a pure aesthete was less in demand.

As the world settles into an economic crisis, architects face another crisis of legitimacy. No one is hiring us, because times are tight and our value is suspect. We would all seek to answer this suspicion in our own ways, but to do so we would need to *practice*. We need to get that commission before we can validate our own claims of our usefulness.

This crisis of validity extends well beneath our current crisis of unemployment. The resolution of the latter will not ensure the resolution of the former. Even as architects go back to work, they face a world where their usefulness will be even more suspect. Their choices will be even narrower and more forced. What a young architect faces today is not merely the specter of unemployment but the knowledge that, even when that particular hurdle is overcome, the great promises of the profession have unraveled. The architect will no longer be in a position of authority, no longer free to create and explore in a meaningful way.

Undoing this reality and reclaiming our authority are more important than employment. Attending to the former ensures the latter. No one can give back to architecture the cultural authority that has been lost, but it can be found again. To gain back that cultural authority, we need to nurture a world where an architect's value is understood prima facie. When we do, we give ourselves our authority back. It is this act—the act of empowerment—that should be our aim. When we empower ourselves, we acquire or develop the skills necessary to enable our own visions of architecture—to be the architects that we want to be. An empowered architect merely seeks to be the master of the forces that typically frustrate us.

3 | The Case for Empowerment

Every individual out there wants to be empowered. That is, we want our own authority to grow. We want more creative freedom, or more money, or more clients, or better clients, or more laurels, or any of the things that come with empowerment. Whatever our motives, to be empowered increases our ability to act on those motives and actualize our aspirations. To be an empowered individual seems fairly straightforward; the question is then: Why, *as a profession,* do we need to be empowered? Why do we need the architectural profession to be empowered as opposed to just having an architectural profession with a few empowered individuals?

I found the answer in the work of a long-ago teacher. As an undergraduate, I had the fortune to take an introductory biology class with Dr. Kenneth Miller. In the years since then, Dr. Miller has emerged as a national advocate not only for the teaching of evolution in science classrooms, but for prohibiting the teaching of intelligent design, creationism, and other such explanations of the origins of life. He has offered his services as an expert witness in Cobb County, Georgia and Dover, Pennsylvania, or seemingly wherever these issues go to court.

Many years after I was in Dr. Miller's class, a friend sent me a clip on YouTube of one of Dr. Miller's recent lectures. In this lecture, which occurred at Case Western University, he described giving a lecture at Harvard detailing his battles in the name of science. At some point, a student proposed a straightforward question: "Who cares what they teach kids in Alabama and Mississippi?" The question was not "Who cares about science?" but "Who cares about these people who don't care about science?" Implied was the idea that science would always prevail, that there would always be champions of science. Harvard would never substitute teaching intelligent design for evolution, and in that sense evolution would always be safe, at least at Harvard.

Dr. Miller's response was, "Damn straight it matters what we teach children in every classroom in this country," and he cited the case of E. O. Wilson, the preeminent Harvard biologist, who had grown up in Alabama. Dr. Miller remarked that the next E. O. Wilson could be in Alabama right now, and that that makes science education matter, period.

Dr. Miller went on to describe a battle over evolution that took place in Kansas: "When the anti-evolution movement got control of the state board of education, they rewrote the definition of science itself. Not just biology, not just evolution, but *science.*" Specifically, the board changed the definition of science from a process that seeks "natural" explanations for phenomena to one that seeks "more adequate" explanations. The problem with getting rid of the word "natural" is that it inherently opens science up to "nonnatural" explanations, or, put another way, *super*natural explanations.

Dr. Miller had many opponents who advocated a balanced inquiry—even former president George W. Bush had said that he thought students should be exposed to both sides of the "issue."

Dr. Miller cheekily pointed out that when you're discussing the "other side" of a science, you rapidly get into some uncomfortable subjects. The "other side" of chemistry is alchemy. The "other side" of psychology is phrenology. The "other side" of science is often just outright magic or superstition. No parent would advocate teaching magic instead of chemistry, or astrology instead of astronomy, and yet these same parents argue vehemently for the teaching of intelligent design alongside evolutionary theory. Dr. Miller argued that when you stretch the definition of "science" enough to accommodate intelligent design, you open it wide enough to legitimize astrology, pyramid power, new age shamanism, and so on as *sciences*.

Dr. Miller's lecture contained notes of gradualism that struck me as pertinent to architectural practice. What he was arguing—in response to his critics and to the student at Harvard—was that protecting the profession was *everyone's* responsibility. That the profession of science was in clear and present danger—and that by allowing bad science to proliferate anywhere, we invite a threat to good science everywhere. I believe he was arguing that protecting good science in Kansas was *the same act* as protecting good science at Harvard, and that it was every scientist's responsibility—from Nobel Prize winners down to high school science teachers.

Can the same be said of architecture? Is architecture under threat? Who is protecting it? Ostensibly, our professional organizations play that role. But in the public eye, it would seem that the most visible protectors of our name and image are our "starchitects"—the heroes who in so many cases act as our de facto ambassadors to the world. Under their flag, the progress of our profession can be decoupled from the work of rank-and-file architects; from the average, from the everyday. What seems to matter is whether one museum or one skyscraper is a triumph. And if, in the course of executing that triumph, 10,000 terrible houses are built and occupied in some other state far from where we live, we haven't lost anything. If, in the course of erecting that one skyscraper, a thousand-acre slum is grown in a country we've never heard of, we can still claim the trappings of success.

To empower architecture, we first have to realize that every inch matters. Every corner of the built environment matters. Robert Fielden writes,

> It is just as important that we look to the architect to care about and work against the two-mile road that has placed the Walmart five miles out of town as it is to build that Walmart building itself. . . . If there is a challenge that we have as professionals in this country, it is to neutralize the impact from the corporate structure that creates this kind of monolithic design and monolithic culture.[1]

Fielden's protestations against monoculture should not be understood in merely moral terms. If a child grows up with no interaction with the built environment other than toxic, prefabricated housing and Wal-Mart and Home Depot, we limit that child's understanding of the difference between good design and bad design. With no knowledge to work from, the child may grow up to be a builder, or a home buyer, or a legislator, and will live and work as someone who places no value on the built environment. He or she will not know, or respect, or appreciate the power of design.

Does that one child matter? According to Dr. Miller, that one child is just the beginning. That one child could be the next hero of our profession—or could be someone who votes for flawed zoning legislation and allows more terrible buildings to be built, or votes down a bond issue that would have paid for a new museum. Maybe we have been slowly nurturing a society that *doesn't* care about its built environment. Maybe, through our indifference, we have brought this unemployment crisis upon ourselves.

Dr. Miller eloquently makes the case that *what people think about science matters*. It matters what nonscientists think and it even matters what rubes think. It matters not just for the sake of lofty, altruistic ideas about the light of science but out of pure pragmatism, out of selfish concern for the survivability of the profession.

Is the architectural profession at risk? Does it need a defense of the sort described by Dr. Miller? I think clearly yes—the rising tide of economic globalization makes societies more inclined to make financially motivated decisions. And if those societies are making decisions based on finance, then their architects are too, however unwillingly or unwittingly. With the exception of a star-powered few, architects may face only two options: capitulate to the client's financially driven motives, or go without work. The ultimate decisions over the built environment, then, are made by nonarchitects, who can easily drive stalwart architects from the table. Any architect who still has a seat at the table makes merely superficial, stylistic decisions.

An alarmist could easily describe this turn of events as the end of our profession—the point at which the public shrugs off what is technical, spiritual, and difficult about architecture and sees us as little more than frosting on the cake. If we are regarded as lowly, our authority will be diminished. With diminished authority, we get fewer chances to earn high regard for our work. The cycle is self-reinforcing, and without a strong professional standing, the authority of the average designer essentially flits to zero.[2]

These prognostications of doom would seem to be at odds with two things: the oldness of the debate, and the previously noted high esteem that architects seem to carry. If things really are that grim, we must at least concede that they have been so for a while. In the late nineteenth century, Viollet-le-Duc proclaimed that "architecture was dying in the bosom of prosperity" and opined that such a decay had in fact been going on since the sixteenth century.[3]

Closer to modern times, Lords Esher and Llewelyn-Davies raised the issue in a RIBA policy document. Addressing issues of fragmentation of skills in the building industry and the need for some supervisory role over all disciplines (a role that now belongs to the professional project management or program management firm), the lords remark:

> There are three reasons why architects should set themselves to provide this comprehensive service. The first is that they are there, trained however imperfectly to think more comprehensively than other relevant disciplines, with a cast of mind that veers habitually (unlike the engineer's) from the particular to the general. The second, less disinterested, is that if they do not achieve this capability they will find themselves sooner than they expected on the fringes of decision-making rather than at the centre, acting as stylists for other people's products. The third is that experience in countries where architects occupy this fringe position, shows that such societies get inferior buildings in every sense of the word.[4]

They gave these warnings in 1968, and there is ample evidence to suggest that they were right—that the grave future they forecast has come to pass. The professions of project management and construction management appear to have cleaved off a significant portion of our responsibilities. Moreover, the emergence of professional project management as a field has erected a wall between the client and the architect, alienating a relationship that had defined us for as long as architecture has been a profession.

Ironically, history usually illustrates that when buildings and the act of building get more complicated, the architect benefits. The emergence of architecture as a professional class seems to have at least some relationship to emergent complexities themselves. One hundred fifty years ago, it was the requirement of literacy that could distinguish an architect from a common mason.[5] In more recent history, it was a literacy in complex code and building systems that could distinguish the architect from his associates in the building trades. When technology surges, the role of the architect is validated.

The last twenty-five years stand as an exception to the historical rule. Buildings have become enormously more complicated—in their systems and tectonic complexity, but more so in their financial, political, and legal trappings. The *act* of building is more complicated; there are increased numbers of stakeholders, all of them potential litigants. There is increased influence and involvement by the financial classes, because the money we use to finance buildings is borrowed, and subject more to interest rates than to capital constraints. As the act of building has become more complicated, architecture in many ways has shrunk from that complexity. This retreat has allowed the professions of project management and construction management to fully develop. It assumed, mistakenly, that there was something strategic in focusing on what we were really good at and/ or really interested in: the professional production of schematic designs and construction documents. This latest surge in technology has only served to validate the existence of *other* professions. Around the time the lords published their "Lords' Prayer,"

Richard Llewelyn-Davies published his famous diagram illustrating the architect's relationship to surrounding professions. I have taken the liberty of updating Llewelyn-Davies's diagram, to show how the architect's sphere of influence has not only shrunk but in some places been overrun.

On the other hand, the profession marches on—and architects have been more and more visible with each decade. Far from being on the fringe, they are on the cover of *Time* magazine and on the trendiest evening talk shows. Is this the grave new world that Esher and Llewelyn-Davies forecast? If our authority has been diminished, why are we seen as the sexiest profession? Why do con men impersonate *us* when they want to get the girl?

At this point, it is important to raise a distinction between being well regarded for what we do, and being well regarded for what we don't do. Consider an experience shared by most architects: being engaged in casual conversation at a bar or a cocktail party and hearing from someone, "I always wanted to be an architect. I was just no good at [blank]." The blank, in this case, can be any number of things, but the most usual suspects are:

(a) Math,

(b) Drawing,

(c) Drafting,

(d) Painting.

Implied in this exchange is that people think that I am good at these things, or that architecture necessarily involves these things. I usually respond with:

(a) Well, I am good at math, but I don't use it and you don't need it to be successful at architecture. For most architects, being able to add two and two and *not* get ten is sufficient.

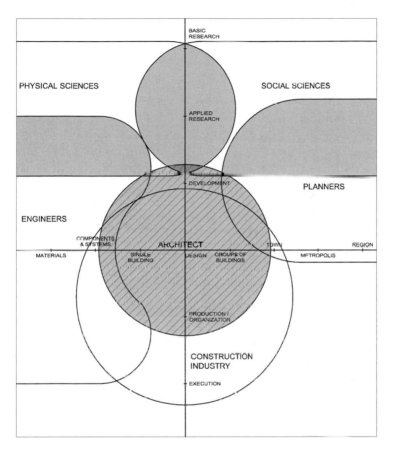

Figure 3.1
Richard Llewelyn-Davies, diagram showing the architect's relation to other professions (1967).

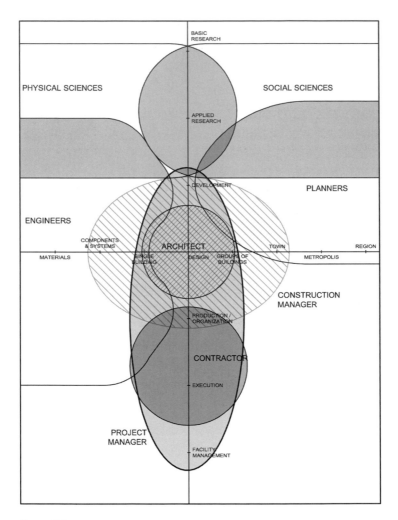

Figure 3.2

The author's imagined updating of Llewelyn-Davies's diagram (2009).

(b) I like sketching, and I *used* to be good at it. It can be central, but there are plenty of architects who get by without it.

(c) The draftsmen usually do the drafting.

(d) What?

What should be becoming clearer is not so much that people have a negative or positive view of the architect, but that they have myriad views. At the time of writing, a commercial for a well-known plumbing fixture company is in heavy rotation. The commercial opens with an architect, dressed dashingly in a black suit and a black turtleneck, leading a couple through a gleaming white office past models and sleek photographs. The voiceover describes all the architect's distinctions and awards. At the end of the commercial, the architect sits in an elegant chair, a distinguished crown of white hair set off against his black suit, and with a face of vague disinterest, asks the young couple "Now what can I do for you?" The woman of the couple pulls a gleaming commercial sink fixture out of her purse, slams it down on the table and demands, "Design something around this!" The commercial fades out on the architect's cocked eyebrows.

Clearly, pop culture does not hold us in high esteem, if it suggests that a plumbing fixture could be the conceptual basis of our work. In my earlier years, I wouldn't have been too pre-occupied with the fact that Madison Avenue was looking down on architects, but in light of the Great Wake I realized that Madison Avenue was commenting on a wider phenomenon. It wasn't telling people what to think about architects, it was reflecting what people *already* thought about architects. It was capitalizing on a widely held perception.

The more *highly* people regard architecture, the more power we have—this much is surely true, and architects of recent generations have understood this. But how *widely* people regard architecture also matters. Not because we are slaves to some idealistic modernist sensibilities, but because these are the people who produce our commercials, who elect our presidents, who vote on referendums and run the PTA—and the fact that they will never, themselves, engage the services of an architect does not mean that they do not have a hand in the destiny of our profession. Pierre Pellegrino puts it more poetically:

> While not all those who use the language of architecture to grasp the world they live in are necessarily poets, the mere fact of living in a product of architecture is an exercise in that language, just as reading a text implies a command of the language in which it is written: a command that is not necessarily as learned as the writer's, but sufficient for the writer to be to some extent understood. And so everyone learns a little about how to write; the Prince is no longer the sole reader of architecture.[6]

This flies in the face of a certain conventional wisdom which holds that to be a critically successful architect, you must gain the adoration of your fellow architects, but not necessarily of your clients and certainly not of the general public. A provocative work of architecture may just as well turn the public off anyway, as happened with Kallmann, McKinnell and Knowles's Boston City Hall—a building which has had an up-and-down history, to say the least. Despite a near universal panning by its users and by Bostonians in general, the building continues to attract accolades (or at least sympathy) from architects.

It may even be said that this tendency to accept the approval of the architectural community, while comfortably distancing oneself from the need for any wider approval, has become institutionalized. Jack Nasar makes the case that Peter Eisenman's winning design for the Wexner Center at Ohio State was, in fact, not the entry most favored by the public. When asked to evaluate the entries against the descriptors of the winning entry provided in the jurors' statement, a cross section of students and faculty uniformly chose Eisenman's entry fourth by those criteria and Arthur Erickson's entry first. The study's authors took selections from the jury's statement that had been written to describe Eisenman's entry (e.g., "is adventurous and challenging" and "takes particular advantage of the site") and asked respondents to evaluate the competition entries against those claims.[7] According to the public, Eisenman's entry was only the fourth best in those terms, but the larger question is: *Who cares?* The jury and the public are *supposed* to have different opinions. The jury is composed of architectural experts, and just as we wouldn't allow normal citizens to make their own medical decisions, we shouldn't allow them to make their own architectural decisions.

The difficulty with this idea is that it presupposes a powerlessness on the part of the public. It shouldn't. The public is not without its arsenal. In the case of the Wexner Center, for example, we have a *public* building, at a *public* university, financed in some part by *public* money, and yet the jury selects an entry that the public finds unsatisfactory. There is no doubting the symbolic and stylistic power of the Wexner Center, but Nasar's study raises the question of whether that symbolic heft translates to anyone besides a small circle of architects. Herbert Gans observes:

> Symbol makers tend to favor high-culture symbols and styles and to forget that the rest of the population may have different symbols. For example, many public buildings follow the dictates of high culture, even though most of the public, which pays for the buildings, does not share these dictates, expressing its feelings in the satirical names that are attached to such buildings.[8]

Name-calling is probably the most innocuous weapon in the public's arsenal. It is true that in the case of the Wexner Center, the public has no direct avenues of appeal. The public cannot cancel the check written to Eisenman, or fire the regents of Ohio State University, or in any direct way sanction those involved in the Wexner Center. What the public can do, however, is *avoid* the building. Alumni, students, or visitors can shun it merely by preferring to spend their time elsewhere. This sends a message to university administrators: *avoid contemporary architecture.* The next time a building is commissioned for the campus, when those administrators again have to make choices about architects and building ambitions, they will do so with the knowledge that a radical, ambitious design will likely go unused by the university community. The Wexner Center cannot be understood in any black-and-white terms. It is certainly a triumph inasmuch as it presented some very new architectural ideas for the first time in built form—a task that is never easy. What is missing from the discussion is an attempt to balance that triumph against the larger question of how such achievements affect the profession as a whole. It has for too long been assumed a priori that the progress of both go hand in hand.

Any progressives, architects or not, should expect challenges to their ideas—indeed the Wexner Center has been heaped since its inception with criticism from a variety of parties. If history has taught us anything, it is that those who aspire to move us beyond our current condition will often be met with such criticism and with unreasonable intractability. However, history also teaches us that great strides forward are eventually redeemed; that at some point the general consciousness catches up to the idea, and what was alien and intrusive is reevaluated and seen as having been progressive. We must therefore look beyond the immediate aftershocks of the leap, to see what legacy it leaves.

It is perhaps too early to write conclusively about the Wexner Center's legacy, although some have already started. Among the possible legacies, the one that should concern us most is if the Wexner Center results in the entire Ohio State community moving away from contemporary architecture. The Wexner is admittedly difficult and expensive to maintain. According to Nasar's research, the building is avoided by most of the campus. Many have publicly declared that it is not an effective space for the display or viewing of art. If the world at large forgives the Wexner Center for these shortcomings and embraces the building anyway, a great service has still been done for architecture. If, on the other hand, the sum of these faults outweighs the Wexner Center's stylistic achievements, we must ask ourselves what victory has been won. If the supposed triumph of the Wexner Center results in a new wave of architectural conservatism at Ohio State, what has been accomplished for architecture? Any future architects who wish to design buildings on the Ohio State campus will have a stark choice: historicist buildings or none at all.

We must defeat the conventional wisdom that an individual victory for one architect or one building is somehow a victory for architecture. It is in the nature of conventional wisdom to be periodically false. Its defining characteristics are only that it be simple, convenient, and comforting. Levitt and Dubner acknowledge that the conventional wisdom isn't *always* wrong, but "noticing where the conventional wisdom may be false—noticing, perhaps, the contrails of sloppy or self-interested thinking—is a nice place to start asking questions."[9]

Architects are not usually known for sloppy thinking. But self-interested thinking? Let us merely say that the architectural profession will give us adequate examples to work with. Our investigation, however, is about empowerment, and not how to chide architects for moments of self-interest. We want to find ways for the architectural profession to prosper as our world economy transitions. We applaud the empowered individuals and their iconic achievements, but in light of this discussion we must ask whether architecture as a profession is in a better place because of them. Has the surge in their power and design authority come at the expense of something more important? Have they stripped from future generations the ability to actualize their own ambitions? In exploring this question, we'll start with the most obvious question: where do we get power in the first place?

4 | Where We Get Power (Kings, Not Sorcerers)

Imagine two men vying for power: a king, and a sorcerer. The king is, of course, the titular head of the realm, and as far as anyone outside the court is concerned, the king is in charge. Inside the court, however, the politics are a little more complex. Everyone, including the king and the sorcerer, is aware that the king relies on the sorcerer for advice and, in a strange way, legitimacy. In a superstitious time, the sorcerer is the king's link to the mystical and the divine. When the queen, or a knight, or a duke or a serf asks the inevitable "Why?" the king can reply with "The sorcerer said so." The sorcerer's judgment is beyond reproach, because no one knows the sorcerer's art.

When a decision is made to go to war, the king might select the enemy, he might call upon his dukes and knights to assemble. He would certainly pony up the gold to pay for the effort. But would he go to war without his sorcerer? No, of course not. He would need his sorcerer's blessing, which would carry with it the implicit approval of the gods, the fates, the furies, or whomever the realm was inclined to worship.

Does this mean that the sorcerer is in charge? Not exactly. The king has a power base that extends from his heredity, military might, cultural inertia, etc. Depending on which king we're talking about, these advantages might have been received at birth, or fought for. But to retain power, the king must act in a certain way. Weak or stupid kings are easily dethroned by more talented or more ambitious aspirants.

One could write many pages on the relationship between kings and their sorcerers, but the critical difference here is *how* they derive their power. The king does so through the observable, the sorcerer through the opaque.

A sorcerer draws his strength from the fact that people *don't* know what he's doing. He mixes some newt's tongue and some bat blood, and some fantastic result occurs. If Disney hasn't been lying to me, there's smoke and mystery and probably some spooky sounds. The sorcerer's process is, *by necessity*, not a process that is repeatable or explainable; if it were, everyone could have the sorcerer's power. We watch the sorcerer and are somehow convinced that the reason these methods seem so impregnable to us is because we are not privy to his power and special skills. Surely we could not recreate the sorcerer's results in our own kitchen, even assuming that we could lay our hands on ogre teeth and owl eyes. We would surely forget some secret, magical ingredient that the sorcerer adds to work his magic! In a way, what *doesn't* make sense about the sorcerer's process is what gives it legitimacy. If it made sense, or was repeatable, then everyone would be a sorcerer.

In modern times, the idea of a man mixing animal body parts together and divining the will of the gods seems absurd. We look back on the time of kings and sorcerers and can easily render the sorcerer as a charlatan—a man who kept a veil of mystery around what he was doing in order to achieve some measure of power or influence. Yet it's just as easy to suppose that the sorcerer, and everyone around him, honestly believed in all that hocus-pocus, and we should be careful not to oversimplify the situation with our modern eyes. It might therefore be easier to think in terms of our modern-day sorcerers. I'll use this word for anyone whose process is uncomfortably opaque. The IT guy, for instance.

I know enough about computers to use them. But like most of us, I'm compelled to use the services of "the IT guy" from time to time. I call upon him when my computer is broken, and he comes around, waves his magic wand, and usually the computer is working again. I don't know anything about his process: was the fix easy? Difficult? Was it a problem that I created? A bug? A glitch? Did the guy even do anything? Who knows? The only thing I know is that there was a problem, and now there's not one. Or perhaps there is a different problem. Anyone who has ever engaged the services of "the IT guy" has scratched his or her head about the IT guy's usefulness. A lot of us have banged our heads in frustration at our own dependency. But at the end of the day, there are too many complexities associated with the computer for us to do without the IT guy. Or we think there are. The IT guy's process is impregnable, and the subject of his tinkering is a mystery. The IT guy is every bit a sorcerer.

A king is quite different. He draws his power in a completely different way. There are obvious issues of heredity and feudal structure, but since this is a metaphor, we will ignore them. A king, if he wishes to avoid usurpers and coups, must command the respect of his knights and subjects. He must inspire loyalty and adoration. A bad king may hold on to his power, but only through bribery, or through convention. Generally a king must be a good king in order to endure.

A king proves himself to be a good king through those qualities we associate with leadership: integrity, honesty, benevolence, empathy, wisdom, etc. The key here is not just possessing those qualities but *demonstrating* them. Publicly, so as to encourage appreciation and loyalty. In feudal times, a king might not necessarily need the support of every serf, but he would require the support of most of the knights and lords of the realm.

One might ask how an architect is supposed to publicly demonstrate his skills when what we do is so complicated—a result of years and years of training. How can we *not* be opaque? After all, an architect, like any professional, operates as an expert. That is, there are things that we are expected to know beyond what the general public knows or what could be obtained casually. This knowledge is extensive enough and specific enough that the government licenses our ability to represent ourselves as experts in this field. Being an expert, however, is a morally neutral designation; it merely describes an asymmetry of information. How an expert behaves is merely a question of incentives. An architect's incentives and the interests of that architect's clients are not necessarily in line. They may, in fact, be diametrically opposed. *But they need not be concealed.*

The tension between bar owners and bartenders is instructive here. Everyone has a favorite bar, and most people have a favorite bartender. While usually not a walking pile of clichés like Sam from *Cheers*, our favorite bartender knows our drink, is welcoming when the rest of the world isn't, and seems wise beyond possibility. Different qualities can earn a bartender his status as favorite, but in the life of a young architect, a long pour goes a long way.

A "long pour" is a euphemism for adding extra alcohol to cocktails. A standard cocktail contains one ounce of liquor. A one-ounce shot of liquor is poured in exactly four seconds. Therefore, if a bartender were to count to five when pouring your drink, it would mean you got 25 percent more alcohol, without having to pay for it. Nothing endears bartenders to me more. As a young architect, I've spent most of my life consistently agitated, often heartbroken, and occasionally unemployed. A stiff drink is mine, by rights.

My favorite bartender knows this, as much as he knows I'm not alone. *Lots* of people like long pours. What's more, the more drunk they get, the more likely they are to order even more drinks, and to tip even more generously. Long pours are good business. For the bartender, that is. For the bar *owner*, it's a terrible proposition. Someone is giving away 20 percent of his inventory for free. The bartender is earning the benefit (in the form of tips) while the owner is paying the cost. The owner may realize some indirect benefit, in the form of a returning customer, but generally speaking it's in the bartenders power to give away a lot more than the bar owner can ever get back.

Here, two professions interact with diametrically opposed incentives. The bartender has an incentive to overpour, the bar owner has an incentive to have him "pour level." And yet they both *know* this and achieve a détente. Most bar owners will regard long pouring as a firing offense; they show very little charity to that sort of behavior. The bartender knows this, and is thus clear about his carrots and sticks. He can make his own assessment about the gains (tips) versus the risks (getting fired). In turn, the bar owner realizes the bartender's position, and can make his own decisions about risks and gains—if he fires the favorite bartender, he will lose a lot of customers; if he doesn't, he may lose a lot of alcohol.

The interactions between an architect and his or her client do not always have this transparency—they can't. To a certain extent, the things we do as architects will remain mysterious, and no one who has not gone through our training will understand them. But it is enough to declare and identify that our interests, as architects, are in line with the interests of society. We cannot always be clear about *how* we do what we do, but we can be clear about *why* we do what we do, and its results should speak to our motives.

Architects should be kings, not sorcerers. Our power should extend from transparent appraisal and demonstrable abilities. This isn't as radical as one might think, because *most* of what we do is not all that mysterious. As Witold Rybczynski points out in discussing scale, there are simple, nonmystical ways to think about architecture:

> There is nothing magic in this question of human dimen-sions. . . . It is, rather, a matter of *fit*. Things can be put down, seen, sat on, sat in, leaned against comfortably. A door is where the person goes through; it is obviously big enough, yet not needlessly larger. It fits.[1]

This simplicity is not always favored, however. In fact, as we stride into a new century, architecture seems to be getting more complex. More and more architects are calling for additional competencies that have strange, techno-sounding names: net-work culture, scripting, etc. These processes find their roots in the very development of the information age itself. The inven-tion of the computer, and the resulting technological devel-opment, represents the fastest and most aggressive period of innovation in mankind's history. Creative energies have poured into the IT field, and a brave new world has been spun out of it. Many of the new design methods in the field of architecture build heavily on this success. Each one is presented as the new panacea that's going to rescue our profession from our current perceived lack of direction. Similar to the way early modernist architects found comfort in how engineers designed, architects look to these new methods to provide not only the means but the direction of our new profession.

Depending on how mystical-sounding the field, we are arguably getting farther away from the simplicity and accompanying transparency that Rybczynski describes. Beyond issues of simplicity and transparency, the trouble with this thinking is that it seemingly suffers from the profession's tendency to overestimate its capabilities. There is often a tendency to believe that the design thinking process is a foolproof methodology—that it can be used to solve any problem, that competencies in architecture are transferable to other activities. Architects find themselves designing everything from teakettles to whole cities. They do so in the belief that design is a cognitive process and a problem-solving methodology, and can be applied as easily to molehills as to mountains. To increase our transparency, we should always be clear about the limits of our abilities.

Where, then, are the limitations of architects' abilities? Clearly, there are Annie Chois out there who think we don't contribute anything and that our skills are useless. But if we had to decide for ourselves, where would we draw the line between what we can do and what we can't?

The tale of planning and urban design is instructive here. If you're not in the field, the distinctions between the professions of urban planning and urban design are probably unknown to you. If you are in the profession, the differences have probably ceased to be particularly important to you—if you favor one, it's probably your own; if you don't, you might not see too severe a distinction in the first place.

Although the border between these two professions can be blurry, both fields concern themselves with the designing and organization of space at an urban scale. There are architects who understand urban design as a subdiscipline of architecture, and there are others who regard it as a hybridization of architecture and landscape/urban principles. There are also those who see urban design as a subdiscipline of planning and those who see it as an entirely separate endeavor. For the sake of discussion, let's examine two specific examples:

If you were to enroll in a master's in urban planning program, the curriculum might look like this:[2]

Core classes:
- Evolution of urban structure
- Planning concepts and controversies
- Research methods for planners
- Quantitative methods for planners

Three of the following electives:
- Economics
- Law and legal systems
- Physical and spatial relations
- Political process/public policy

One planning studio

If you were to enroll in an urban design program, your education would be quite different. The bulk of your time and energy would be spent in design studio—making diagrams, drawings, models, etc. Your educational agenda might include a specific interest in regionalism, place-making, urban culture, etc.:

Three full design studios (with an additional, optional international studio):
- Race, class, gender
- Theories of urban design

- History of urban form
- Methodologies of urban design
- Additional electives

Within those electives and seminar classes, you might find content like the following:[3]

- Signature moments and movements in the history of urban design and city-making
- Criticisms of modern planning and design
- Theoretical concepts of place
- Place-making practices
- Typology and morphology in urban design
- Physical form—implications and externalities
- Physical elements of urban design
- Urban design practice
- The future is now

Even to a nonarchitect, the differences should be obvious. Planning deals with "research" and the "quantitative," while the urban design degree deals with the "theoretical" and "form implications" of urbanism. If you had an interest in the city, and wanted to be a shaper of cities, you might ask yourself which field you should get into. You could go into either one—they both hold sway over our urban form. But clearly they each have limitations as well. An urban designer may not be well versed in the legal theory of cities—how zoning legislation gets passed, and how much it affects the ultimate built form of our cities— as is his planning colleague. On the other hand, a planner is not traditionally versed in design methods. Planners may not be aware of the theoretical and philosophical underpinnings of our urban choices. They may, therefore, make poor ones. To resort to classical stereotypes, perhaps planners are the pragmatists and urban designers are the poets.

Setting aside those efforts to bleed the two disciplines together, it would seem that there is nothing particularly wrong with this sharing of influence between them. Psychologists and psychiatrists both attend to our mental health—but they are trained very differently and practice differently as well. Perhaps we are better off as a result of the fact that two very different professions and cultures collide to design our cities. The only danger, it would seem, occurs when one of the professions grows contented in its half-knowledge. If planners suddenly decided that urban designers had nothing to offer, or vice versa, we might see our cities suffer as a result.

To the extent that both professions avoid this turn of events, it means that they remain cognizant of the limitations of their own knowledge. They know what they don't know. I'd like to think that architects are the same—but I know a lot of architects (among them, myself). Because of the ways in which architects are trained, incomplete knowledge is often no barrier to a complete design. A design's function is merely to *convince*. This often lulls us into self-deception—especially where reality is too complicated or aggravating. We cease to be transparent, even to ourselves.

As designers, we have the ability to conduct our work in a way that deceives the client as well as ourselves. Both in the academic world and the professional world, architects have many incentives to obscure any half-knowledge. We are called upon to be experts in situations where we're clearly not, and we are sanctioned for demonstrating understandable ignorance. We are *pushed* into being sorcerers.

It is this tendency that is the disconcerting heart of our evolving practice. While technology surges, new methods are even more opaque than the previous ones. In many ways, the architecture community's recent interest in parroting the design methods of the IT community seems very similar to its interest in parroting the design methods of the engineering community a century ago. Then, architects liked the way engineers designed, because in the absence of a definitive style like Gothic or rococo, engineering design methods offered clarity. To embrace industry and engineering was to find shelter from the chaos brought by a multitude of historical styles jostling for position. Engineers had shown us a way to design, a way that had already produced the greatest innovations of the late nineteenth and early twentieth century.

It seems obvious to us now that there are certain differences in the ways architects and engineers design. *Necessary* differences. Like planners and urban designers, these two professions act on the same stage but do not have the same roles. Likewise, the technology community has plenty of "designers"—they have brought us the Internet, the microwave, and the iPhone. Technology may yet be the driving force in society, even though it is now wrought of silicon and light rather than steel and flame. Despite its centrality to our society, technology has its limits. The traditional design of a bridge requires a certain mentality: you have to cover the span of a canyon, or a river. As long as you cover that span, there are definitive ways to distinguish between a *good* bridge and a *bad* bridge. In engineering terms, a good bridge is the one that is the cheapest, or uses the least amount of materials, or gets done the fastest. Designing a microchip operates on similar principles. There's some accounting for taste in consumer products, but the march of demand has always focused on what is smaller, faster, cheaper, and more powerful.

But neither the bridge nor the microchip represents the standards by which we judge architecture. We expect architecture to perform differently. We expect architecture to comfort us, to reassure us, to remind us, and to describe us. It operates on different principles and should therefore not be confused with some broader definition of design.

That being said, it will be necessary in the future for architects to design more than they do. We will not necessarily design anything other than buildings, but our sphere of knowledge and influence will need to increase. It certainly cannot erode any further. As designers, we will need to make choices that acknowledge and surmount the world's new challenges. We will have to come to hard truths about the limits of what we do, and then leap beyond those boundaries. To grow after the Great Wake, we need to be ten architects:

(1) The financial architect

(2) The value architect

(3) The risk architect

(4) The paid architect

(5) The idea architect

(6) The knowing architect

(7) The named architect

(8) The citizen architect

(9) The green architect

(10) The sober architect

Like many parents, my father occasionally had to go into the office on weekends. On the occasions when too little notice was given, he couldn't find a babysitter and I got an impromptu field trip downtown. At four or five, "downtown" wasn't really that impressive. Sure, it was different, but at that age I was still inclined to find giant, transforming robots at the center of my attention, and since downtown D.C. had none of those, I would have been content to stay home and watch cartoons. Nonetheless, I would good-humoredly accompany my father downtown because of the fish. Going downtown on a Saturday always meant a detour to the fish market. My dad would buy a whole fish—usually a bluefish—which we would take home and prepare. Fish guts were a close second to giant robots in my hierarchy of cool. Gutting a fish was serious business, especially when the selected fish rivaled my tiny body in size. The stomach was always full of little crabs and fish parts, and for a five year old, it was a cool way to spend an afternoon.

On one of these particular Saturdays, we were on the way back, bluefish in hand, when we passed an abandoned, boarded-up house. In the front yard a homeless man had made camp, assembling a shelter of boxes, newspapers, and debris. I think I remember a few milk crates woven into the construction, spotting it with bright moments of red. He had made what appeared to my five-year-old eyes very much like *a fort. Only it was better than the forts that my sister and I used to make by pushing the couches together. This fort was weatherproof and outside. It had a sturdiness about it, a permanence which, had I been an adult, I would have found tragic. But at five I was inspired, because he had managed to combine two of my favorite things—fort making and camping. I informed my father that upon our return home, I would not be assisting with the gutting of the fish. I was going straightaway to start assembling my front yard camping-fort, and he was welcome to assist me. I pointed to the man and expressed my astonishment—all this time, I could have been camping in the front yard of our house. I cannot ever remember being more resolved about anything in my young life. My dad responded like a father does—with the bad news:*

Dad: *That man is not camping, he's homeless.*

Me: *Why doesn't he live in his house?*

Dad: *That's not his house.*

Me: *Well, who lives in the house?*

Dad: *Nobody lives in the house. The man that owns the house doesn't live there. He lives somewhere else, that's why all the windows were covered with plywood.*

Me: *Why doesn't he let the camping man live there if he's not using it?*

Dad: *Because the camping man can't pay rent.*

Me: *What's rent?*

Dad: *It's when you pay your allowance to someone so that you can live at their house. The camping man has no allowance.*

After that the discussion turned a bit technical. My father refused to infantilize my sister and I, so he always did his best to speak to us like grownups. This worked well in explaining the birds and the bees, or how a car worked, but not so much in explaining the macroeconomic basis for blight. I can't remember exactly what his explanation was, but

I remember it being inadequate to my young ears. I remember the first stirrings of the moral indignation that would later spell my greatest triumphs and my greatest failings. Whatever the explanation was, I never got over it. How could homelessness and blight coexist in the same society, in the same city, on the same lot? It seemed to defy all logic.

I didn't intend to, but I proceeded at that point to drop the hammer on my father: "Can the camping man come live with us?"

I can't even remember how my dad answered that one. I shudder to think. I know that at the time I found his explanation inadequate again. Every explanation since then has been equally unsatisfactory. In some ways, it formed the basis of my initial interests in architecture and the built environment. Later, this episode would frame much of my thinking about the inextricable links between finance and the built environment.

6 | The Financial Architect (or, A Brief Economic History of Architecture)

I accord the financial architect primacy among the ten architects because of the way that money and finance have come to dominate conversations about the built world. Where once there was room for craft, we now feel compelled to justify every cent spent. Everyone wants more for less. We have become a culture that embraces *things* and *stuff,* and the more we have of them, the better. Our present economic crisis is in some way a derivative of these instincts, but our recovery will paradoxically sharpen them.

There is a sense today that we have been ripped off—by Wall Street, by Washington, by our own selves. In the future, we will make choices that are even more concerned about value, transparency, and permanence. We will eschew the opaque, the immediate gratification, and the glitzy. This transition will be muddy, because even when we take a stand against consumer culture, we seemingly embrace it at the same time. But whether we embrace or reject this dollar-driven culture, we will certainly need to know much more about it—that's why the financial architect comes first.

Our story centers on the eighties. America became a finance nation in the eighties because of the way the country changed economically, then culturally, and finally architecturally. For the roots of this change, however, we have to go back several decades further, to the period between the world wars and the rise of modernism in architecture. Modernism represented a complete break in the way architecture was practiced—a fact that is often overlooked because of the formal changes that were equally dramatic. But the most significant change brought by modernism was not the kind of architecture that was made, but *how* architecture was made.

In a sense, modernism brought egalitarianism to architectural practice. In classical architecture, the methods were reasonably structured. There were a certain number of orders and details one could be required to know. Clients expected traditionalism in designs. Therefore, *getting* work was not necessarily about coming up with a brilliant idea or putting out something original. One's success in getting work had much more to do with external factors, such as one's place in society, specifically one's connectedness to the existing circles of wealth and power.

Arguably, the same conditions exist today, but, at least philosophically, modernism implied something different. It implied that great architecture came out of rigorous application of rules and theory—that architecture, like science, math, and engineering, could be logically *divined*.

The implications of this change were massive. In the same way that the next great mathematical theorem could come from class-blind brilliance, so too could the new architecture. In mathematics and engineering, good work was good work, and there were objective means of establishing what was right and what was wrong. If a brilliant new theorem arrived from the mind of an undergraduate, or a street pauper, or the scion of a wealthy family, the brilliance of the idea would be no more or less brilliant on account of its origins. An idea from humble beginnings might even attract more attention because of its romantic qualities.

Modernism itself had its share of "starchitects," but its underlying structure would ensure that starchitecture would become a permanent fixture in the profession. As in the movies or professional sports, the only way to attract individuals to the profession and to convince them to put up with its long hours, low wages, and high riskiness is to hold before them the possibility of upward mobility. They must believe that the zenith of the profession is within their reach—a possibility that existed under modernism but not within classical architecture. By convincing people that they might become stars, we ensure that they will be content with the fact that, for now, they are not stars. By creating a profession where many architects don't achieve fame and financial security until well into their fifties or sixties, we ensure that architects in their thirties and forties will not demand as much. They must believe that the constant and rigorous application of their craft will one day be rewarded. In modernism, great architecture would be the result of great methods, not great social standing. As such, the zenith was within reach of everyone, at least theoretically. Culturally, this is consistent with the postwar period in both America and Europe, a period of incredible industry and faith in the rewards of hard work.

The unwinding of this optimism is our national story, though not necessarily the subject of this book. Payola, Watergate, and the Vietnam War all worked to undermine the rosy, formulaic ideas of rightness and success that Americans had constructed. We came to understand that good guys don't always win, bad guys don't always get caught, and sometimes hard work and good life don't go together. A parallel, similar unwinding was ongoing in architecture in the form of postmodernism. Post-modernism was chipping away at the rules that modernism had set out for us, and in so doing chipped at the foundations of the utopia that modernism had promised to deliver.

More change, culturally and architecturally, would follow as we moved into the eighties, when Reaganomics and deconstruc-tivism evolved together. It is sufficient to observe that over the last thirty years we got to *feeling* wealthier—fast. The wealth was not evenly distributed—in fact, most of the population was not seeing any real gains. But easier and easier credit allowed us to *feel* wealthier. Seemingly, we needed some place to put all of that money. A generation ago, this was never a problem—most people never had the burden of having a lot of extra money around, so they never had to worry about what to do with it. As our disposable incomes and our credit lines increased, people wanted something to do with their money.

A prosperous society will find increasingly frivolous ways to spend its money. There was the inevitable attraction of con-sumer products. The difficulty with consumer purchases is that they represent a negative investment. We buy a big fancy televi-sion, it affords us some satisfaction, but this is fleeting. The tech-nology fades, and the television is only really satisfying until the neighbor buys a bigger one.

For finance and economic wonks, 1973 stands out as a wa-tershed: the year when American growth stopped. America's economy and standard of living had been rising, sometimes dramatically, every year since the end of the World War II. 1973 was marked by the first big rise in the price of oil after the Yom Kippur War, a relaxation of fixed exchanged rates, and a double-digit rise in consumer prices.[1] The Federal Reserve Board responded by constricting the money supply, and a recession predictably followed. However, as the economy recovered, American productivity didn't—at least not to its previous levels. At the same time, the seventies saw a steep rise in the regulatory costs of business from programs like the Occupational Safety and Health Administration and the Environmental Protection Agency.[2] Conservatives spent a decade making a case that was starting to seem more and more plausible: that the slowdown in American productivity was because businesses were being over-burdened by regulation, taxation, and inflation. The only way to restore American productivity was to get the government out of America's business.

The Reagan revolution was built on such foundations. Beginning in the 1980s, deregulation in the financial sector gave individuals more and more choices about what to do with their money. Basically, the government gave banks more options about what to do with *their* money, so they were able to create more and more possibilities for what to do with *your* money.

We began to see a migration of the nation's wealth, from savings accounts at the local bank to Wall Street. Again, we're not so much interested in what happened economically, but rather how those economic changes shaped our culture. Ironically, Americans weren't really getting richer. Even by the end of the eighties, the typical family had a real income only 5 percent higher than the typical family in the early seventies—and they achieved that only by working longer hours.[3] But Americans were starting to think seriously about getting rich quick. It seemed more and more plausible.

Perhaps nowhere was this transition more obvious than in the changing of our television tastes. The character of our sixties preferences was consistent: we enjoyed television shows about western adventure (*Wagon Train*), rugged individualism

(*Bonanza*), the mockery of wealth (*Beverly Hillbillies*), and small town folksiness (*The Andy Griffith Show*). Our taste in the seventies was different, but held a similar internal consistency. We enjoyed blue-collar heroism (*All in the Family, Laverne & Shirley*) and nostalgia for simpler times (*Happy Days*). During the eighties, our tastes changed dramatically. The most watched television series of the year always had to do with the good life, except for the 1982–83 season, when *60 Minutes* took the top slot. In all other years it was *Dallas, Dynasty*, or *The Cosby Show*. *The Cosby Show* seemed to signal a transition: from a fascination with wealth to a comfort with it. The wealthy were no longer depicted as melodramatic backstabbers but as good, folksy neighbors, who just happened to be a doctor and a lawyer, interestingly enough.

We knew, intimately, what the wealthy life was like, and it seemed within our grasp.

The most ubiquitous architectural outgrowth of this cultural evolution was the McMansion phenomenon. It was the most pervasive expression of our new wealth culture. It did not, of course, represent real wealth. In many cases, the buildings were hastily constructed—a rapidly produced pastiche designed to give old-money validation to new-money (or new-credit) buyers. Lot size generally remained the same; even if you got that estate look, you probably couldn't afford the estate to go with it. But homes are appraised by square footage, and there was at least some perceived correlation between an increased square footage and the wealth that was being paraded on television.

A more dramatic expression of eighties wealth culture was deconstructivism itself. Deconstructivism is fundamentally an architecture of the rich. At first blush, it might seem the most democratic and egalitarian of formal styles. Many regard Gehry's

Santa Monica house as one of the earliest deconstructivist buildings, and it was assembled from homely and everyday materials.
The only richness about it is in its creativity and bravado. However, we would expect an "architecture of the rich" to exhibit
certain qualities, and they would likely be the same qualities
that we observe in rich people or rich societies. We would likely
see incidents of conspicuous consumption, or a downplaying
of utility. As an individual or a society grows richer, the need
to justify, to oneself or anyone else, the reasoning behind one's
purchases becomes remote. The need to worry about utility, durability, or sensibility fades, because worrying is a tacit confes-
sion of poverty. In this society, $4 for a cup of coffee begins to
sound reasonable.

We have already said that the eighties were much more about
seeming rich than *being* rich, and in order to seem rich, one must
conspicuously renounce utilitarianism. One must revel in the
superfluous. People were doing it on TV and in the movies; the
Sharper Image arrived at the local mall. Consumption was *in*.
However, there is a limit to how much disposable income one
can spend on lattes. Investing began to creep into the public
consciousness as the next logical act of consumption. What
better way to dispose of your disposable income? Rather than
spending it on fleeting consumer products or letting it lie dor-
mant in the local farmer's bank, you could send it to Wall Street.
There, if you played your cards right, your money could make
more money *out of itself*, pay for your kids' college education,
and leave plenty left over to keep you in lattes throughout your
early retirement.

The only barrier to this fantasy scenario was the *risk*. Some
people were up for it, some weren't. While Wall Street in the
eighties was a great place to make some money, there were

plenty of average Americans who saw the obvious risk in sending enormous sums to some stranger in another city for investment in something they didn't completely understand. This cautiousness perhaps limited the extent to which economic calamity descended in the eighties.

Not that the eighties was without its scares. The decade had begun in recession and double-digit inflation, and many of us still remember 1987's Black Monday as a rude awakening. Clearly, the market was fraught with risks. However, the risks would be increasingly obviated by a combination of factors, among them our romance with technology and our monetary policy.

People came to believe that we were in a new renaissance, and that continual improvements in technology allowed people to be more and more productive, thereby increasing the economic output of you, me, and everyone. The tech industry seemed to be an investment oasis where the trees grew to the sky. Technology would continue to improve, and we would therefore continually lead happier, healthier, and wealthier lives. There are many measure of economic wellness, but we will think of it this way: if a computer allows you to do what used to be a day's work in four hours, then you ought to be able to do two days' work in a single work day. If you can do that, then you should get paid twice as much. Therefore, the introduction of the computer *doubles* the economic gain that you get from waking up and putting on a tie in the morning. This is an oversimplified example, but people generally believed that the economic benefits associated with technology were going to be widespread, massive, and *continual*.

Unfortunately, we bought into this idea with our monetary policy. A basic rule of human nature is that when the economy is racing, people throw their money at it, desperate to cash in on the prosperity. If the people are not putting enough money into the economy, banks collapse, stock prices drop, unemployment hits, etc. If people are putting too much money into the economy, they drive up prices on some items to fairly silly levels, as happened in the IT boom of the nineties. The Federal Reserve is charged with helping to control how much money people are putting into the economy, so as to avoid irrational panics of two kinds: the kind where people put their money in, and the kind where people pull their money out.

Increasingly, the Fed believed that the investors' faith in a technological panacea was perfectly appropriate. Billions of dollars flowed out of our pockets and into tech stocks not because of an irrational exuberance, but because the American investor knew the real score: technology was going to make us all rich. The Fed allowed this delusion to continue by continually altering the money supply in favor of investment. It *wanted* your money to keep flowing. One can imagine an individual investor sitting at his computer, watching the bubble grow, saying to himself, *Man, this thing is going to burst.* Aware of the investor's anxiety, the Fed responds by dropping the interest rate by half a point. Suddenly, the individual investor's anxiety is overcome. The *gain* to be had by investing at this new, lower interest rate offsets the *potential* loss obvious in the size of the bubble. He forwards more money into the system.

The sum of all these events, from a cultural perspective, is that we blunted our own sense of riskiness. It is the drama of a bar patron who says, "No, no, I've had enough," and an unscrupulous bartender who keeps lowering the price of drinks.

Our postwar culture had embraced hard work and savings. Our eighties culture had told us that we could get rich quick, but there was still far too much risk for all of us to get on the bandwagon. At last in the nineties, through a combination of monetary policy and technology, we watched that risk disappear and threw our hat into the ring. We became a nation of easy, risk-free money. Nowhere was this transition more obvious than in our national savings rate, which peaked at around 15 percent in the late seventies and descended to –3 percent by the time the Great Wake washed ashore.

As our collective economic culture evolved, so too did our architecture. Deconstructivism and eighties capitalism have at their core a similar ideological root. They are about taking daring chances in the face of our own skepticism, about embracing success in the moment instead of the security of the long haul. In a more pragmatic culture, many of the deconstructivist ideas would never have gotten out of the sketchbook. However, in a culture of easy money and sky-high risk tolerance, many things become possible. The bizarre becomes interesting and the irrational becomes avant-garde. We could convince a client that it was important or interesting to make a building that disoriented its visitors or didn't address its own program. We could even convince them that they should spend money on a nonstructural column that doesn't meet the ground. Certain formal decisions only seem palatable when the money we're spending is cheaply obtained—or when it belongs to someone else.

As we are coming to understand, things got worse—a lot worse. Fundamentally, it was because trees *don't* grow to the sky. The IT bubble was bound to burst, and in hindsight we all understand why. People were pulling their money out of the stock market. They would have pulled their money out of the economy completely, except for the collusion, again, of monetary policy against the backdrop of a hunger for risk-free investment.

At the time that Internet stocks were really starting to seem like a bad idea, real estate was starting to seem like a really good idea. Imagine an individual who invests $100,000 in the stock market in, say, 1995. By 1999 that person might have easily turned that $100,000 into $500,000. By 2000, however, that $500,000 might only be worth $400,000. In a panic, the investor yanks his or her money out of the stock market (thus, incidentally, contributing to the market's free fall), but *where to put the $400,000?* You can't just leave $400,000 in cash lying around. A house or a condo at this point would seem like a great idea. Real estate is traditionally a safe investment and might give our investor a breather from all the gut-wrenching ups and downs of the stock market. The Fed once again played the enabler, lowering interest rates to as little as 1 percent.

However, the rush to real estate as an investment failed to take into account that we had been *culturally* changed. For the baby boomer generation, a house was a great investment because you put your down payment in (which you had saved for many years), you made your mortgage payment every month, and over the years you built up some very valuable equity. This sort of investing was not of interest to those who had come to economic and professional power during the eighties and nineties. Investing in real estate, in the traditional way, was *boring*. No one wanted to sit around and wait 10 years for a return on their investment. The entire nature of investing had changed. For real estate to be appealing to this new, changed mentality, it would have to offer low risk and a high, fast return. The low interest rates and the Internet wealth pushed us away from the stable, middle-class, home-owning society of a generation before. Instead, we wanted to buy South Beach condos that had not even been built yet. We wanted them so that we could flip them the day after the building opened and double our money. The building industry thought this was brilliant, because it was able to take the money from the presales and use it to fund the construction of the building or of other projects.

With poor values and little respect for our built environment, housing became our new bubble. Like the IT bubble, we believed that it was risk-free. And like the IT bubble, we were greatly assisted by a monetary policy that sought to change our very notion of risk.

While the economic policies of the eighties formed an ideological backdrop for our culture, and thus for our architecture, it was the nineties that did the most damage to our built environment. In the nineties we began to understand our built environment as an *investment* vehicle. In so many circles, the holiness and possibilities of a home, or an office, or a park were removed. How we think about our own environment changed dramatically.

If a house is just an investment vehicle, then the principal concern should be "How much can we get for it later?" In this new economic reality, things like massing and tectonics start to become very unimportant. If we're concerned about resale, then we would do best to focus on only those qualities that are most generic. We would want a house that is as big as possible. With nameless, generic features and conventional detailing. And, of course, location becomes even more important than it already was.

If a man cares about his house and wants to live there, he will want the services of an architect. An architect can tell him how to make a great house *for him*. If this man only sees his house as an investment vehicle, however, then he has little use for an architect. He will want to consult with people who can tell him the most about how to make his house valuable to *other* people. He will seek the counsel of builders, developers, loan officers, and the all-knowing real estate agent.

Consequently, architects participate very little in our domestic housing market. It's not because they don't want to, but because in the last thirty years we have changed all of our economic and cultural expectations of our built environment. So much so that none of the issues on the table are matters of concern to the architect.

All of this might sound quite depressing, except for the fact that it is resoundingly over. The bubble has burst. We have lost a lot of our wealth and hopefully picked up some lessons: not least that any investment vehicle is a bad one, if the only things it promises are short-term, risk-free rewards. In place of this myth, we may get back, as a culture, to more immutable ideas.

This will hopefully be a boon to architectural practice. People will put more value on their built spaces, and the insights of an architect will gain more favor. However, architecture must respond in kind by understanding the basis of that transition. We must understand *why* someone would value our opinion.

A designer's decisions are easily challenged on the basis of finance and money. Everybody wants their *stuff*, and the more of their money you use on their building, the less money they have leftover for stuff. A designer declares, "We need *this* in your building," and the client is inclined to agree, unless the client believes it is too expensive; then the architect's judgment falls into question. Perhaps in no other professional service would you hear such a conversation. If a lawyer tells us that we need *these* five clauses in our will and that it will cost us $500, few of us would be inclined to tell the lawyer, "$500 is too much, and

I don't feel like I need all those clauses. Make it work with four clauses, then I only have to pay $400."

It was such absurdities that fueled my early interest in finance and drove me to business school. I went to understand the languages of business and finance. I wasn't particularly interested in business as such or being a businessperson, whatever that is, but I wanted to understand why and how people who weren't architects made decisions about architecture. What I expected to find was a plethora of techniques and methods, and a dearth of culture and process. To some degree, what I found was the opposite. *Finance is a process*—a means of thinking about the world. Not all that dissimilar from design, actually. It doesn't have anything to do with budgets or costs, but rather with the quantification of nonnumeric and nonmonetary phenomena. Those who study finance at elite levels attempt to quantify such mysteries as risk, time, panic, social thinking. Those who study economics at elite levels are fundamentally trying to understand decision making. None of these seemed to me to be beyond the purview of architecture. To me, finance was merely the study of how things worked—of how to get ideas from the presentation board to the ribbon cutting—and I approached it in that way.

If we care about moving our ideas from the presentation board to the building site, we owe it to ourselves to be masters of the forces that dictate that transition. I was a modernist at heart, and had remembered Gropius teaching us of the need "to make the architect a coordinator of social, psychological, and economic facts, as much as an artist and technologist."[4]

We should care about *everything* that pertains to the ultimate disposition of our design ideas. Within that "everything," finance seemed paramount, or at least as important as some other things that have fallen under the umbrella of "design issues."

Twenty years ago, sustainability was considered "fringe" architecture. It was hardly discussed. Over the course of a few decades, it has worked its way into one of the primary issues of design. Why? Because it became important to society. I similarly reasoned that in our changing professional landscape, issues of finance were going to follow a similar arc.

My opinions on the sympathy between finance and architecture were not terribly widespread, however, and my graduate years were spent trying to understand this cultural gap as much as anything else. My working theory was that the architects I was talking to learned about finance the way I had originally done so—by listening to another architect. Using diatribes from architects many years my senior and periodic conversations with moneyed clients (usually when I was being told to cut costs), I had crafted a (mis)understanding of the financial workings of the world. That misunderstanding dictated that finance and architecture only really have one intersection: cost.

Business school revealed to me that I had been quite wrong about some of what I thought I knew. None of what I learned in business school was at odds with what architecture school had taught me about *architecture*. But most of what architecture had taught me about business was, plainly, incorrect. It might seem arrogant to say that the whole profession of architecture may be nourishing misconceptions about finance and money, until one remembers that our *whole society* has been nourishing misconceptions about finance and money. If Alan Greenspan and Jim Cramer got so much wrong, it might be possible that the architects did too.

Where might all these misconceptions have gotten started? Imagine for a second that you got invited to a dinner party. The hostess, a good friend of yours, is an enthusiastic entertainer and periodically arranges dinner parties for a wide circle of friends and associates, bringing together friends, and sometimes strangers, for lively discussion.

On being invited, you ask the hostess whether there's anything you can bring. She replies, "Well, why don't you bring the beer?" Whether you were given this duty because the hostess thinks that you're great at picking out beer or for some other reason is not quite clear—but you accept the request because you are, in point of fact, great at picking out beer. You're one of those beer aficionados who knows the right beer for every occasion, at least according to your friends.

The evening of the dinner party is upon you, and you procure the evening's libations. You arrive, the table is set, and a good time is had by all. Other guests have brought bread, cheese, appetizers, and wine. A lively conversation is stirred and new friends are made. At least one grudge is settled and at least one other is born. All in all, a typical dinner party. On leaving, you notice that there is a bit of beer left, but in accordance with good manners, you leave it to the hostess.

A month passes, and you are invited to another dinner party. Same circumstances, but a slightly different guest list. Again, because you were raised so well, you inquire whether there is anything you can bring. Again, the response is, "Well, why don't you bring the beer?" Nothing irregular about this comment—you merely take it as a compliment of your prior success in selecting the proper beer. So you bring some more beer and another lively dinner party is written into the history books. In passing, though, you happen to notice again that there is leftover beer, which now falls into the private stock of the hostess.

This scenario repeats itself again and again over the months. You become known as "the beer guy," especially to the hostess.

You bump into her at a PTA meeting and she jokingly asks you why you didn't bring the beer. She begins to refer to you as the "beer guy" amid the dinner party conversation, and whenever the selection is poor or the beer runs out, you are lightheartedly berated.

You can draw only one conclusion from this series of events: *the hostess is a raging alcoholic.* Why else would she constantly be asking you for beer? Why else would she keep the leftover beer—to be drunk in secret and alone? You decide that you have become an enabler. The other guests bring this or that—you don't really know where all the food comes from or even what it is half the time. The only thing you know for certain is that you bring the beer. You also realize that when you confront the hostess about her drinking problem, you probably won't be invited to any more dinner parties. Such is the fate of the noble, right? They stick their necks out and do the right thing, and they're punished for it! But you feel confident in both your analysis of the situation and your remedy for it. You are, after all, the *beer guy.* Who else is better qualified to diagnose alcoholism?

Of course, by now our scenario has started to get a bit silly. If any of our friends acted like this "beer guy" or drew his conclusions, we would assume them to be socially inept, if not downright idiots. The beer guy has taken a few disconnected bits of information and drawn some pretty broad conclusions. Perhaps worse, he has taken some rather specific knowledge (knowledge of beer) and has extrapolated from there to an expert-level knowledge on social behavior, psychology, alcoholism, morality, etc.

For the beer guy and everyone else, it is difficult to accurately draw the boundaries of one's own knowledge. "Seeing what you can't see" is perhaps not possible. Perhaps not even necessary.

What is necessary is for us to be *wary* of what we can't see. We should design around the invisible elephant in the room. In other words, we should try to avoid being the beer guy.

This is not always easy to do as an architect. There are structural forces within the profession that pressure one to be declarative. The circumstances ask us to do the impossible—to act the expert when we know that there is much that we're not seeing. To abolish our insecurities (at least publicly) and wear the hat of the genius. No one wants to hire an architect who's all shrugs and head-scratching; the reward for such honesty would be a dearth of clients.[5] Architects face a trap, and often the only way to surmount the great field of unknowable facts and variables is to set them beyond our concern.

Similarly, the beer guy surmounts the chaos by ignoring it. He chooses not to see that the beer that he was asked to bring was just one aspect of the party. He also chooses to ignore the fact that the other guests were bringing cheese and bread—in other words, making valuable contributions as well. He refuses to understand that a dinner party where only beer is served wouldn't be much of a dinner party (although, admittedly, it would be a much different, possibly better kind of party). He ignores the fact that the hostess has been putting in a lot of effort that never materialized as foodstuffs. The scheduling, the inviting, the hemming and hawing that goes into deciding who might sit next to whom and whether it will breed a lively discussion, a fight, a friendship, or a marriage. The beer guy never confronted the mountain of dishes that were left at the end of the party—and the fact that the hostess was left to do them alone. Finally, the beer guy sets himself out of reach of the aftereffects of the party—gossip and scandal.

In sum, the beer guy has constrained his own perspective. If he had broadened it, he might never have drawn the conclusions that he did; or, he might forgive the hostess for being a functioning alcoholic, given the circumstances.

As architects, we understand buildings. We *know* them, in an intimate way that other professions do not. It is folly, however, to believe that the ways in which we understand buildings are the only ways in which buildings can be understood. It is similarly narrow-minded to reduce all of a client's issues to the one that we confront most directly: cost. We work with owners, owners' representatives, developers, and governments, all of whom have a great number of balls in the air, and assume that the ball that is being hurled at us (cost) is the most important (or the only) ball in play. We arrive at conclusions that are erroneous merely because they are drawn out of that initial misconception.

The clients I know worry about a lot of *stuff*. They worry about rates of return, risk, time, and opportunity costs. The sum of these considerations is "finance." The "cost" of something, in fact, can be made irrelevant by a number of other factors. Whether a project costs a lot, or a little, might not actually matter a whole lot if the rate of return is high relative to the risk, or if the breakeven point is quick relative to a client's other opportunities.

The architect typically does not focus on these issues—they exist primarily within the purview of the client. They are issues that the client analyzes and weighs when consulting with his or her market analyst, or bonding agent, or lender, or financial advisor, or purchaser, or attorney.

Like the other guests at the dinner party, the aforementioned professionals bring *something* to the table. Whether we, as architects, consider what they bring important or not does not change the fact that the *client* thinks it's important or that our fate is changed by their having brought it.

The client collectivizes this information, and his or her decisions are informed by that *collective* pot of information. The weighing of the different ingredients in this pot is the process of finance. Clients are known to harangue architects about costs. This much we all know to be true. That truth, however, in no way demonstrates that this is all that is important to the client. We must defeat the idea, held widely among architects, that the client's only priority is keeping costs down and stymieing the architect's efforts to make "good" architecture. If we can acknowledge that the client's decision-making process is indeed sophisticated and practical, then we can allow our own design processes to grow into that complexity, rather than leaning on caricatures. This does not mean that we do whatever the client wants. There are plenty of those architects and they do us no service. It means, rather, that we make efforts to understand and account for the emergent complexities around us. To move beyond the restrictions imposed by our own perspective, we must challenge our conventional understandings of basic financial ideas, like cost, value, and risk.

The dental work I mentioned in the introduction did not get addressed. At least not the way I envisioned. I had a filling that had fallen out during thesis semester. I declined to get it fixed, owing to a lack of time and money. "Real life" was also just a few short months away, and everything is easier to fix in real life. There is money, free time, insurance, sanity, etc. In the meantime, I had models to build, presentations to give, and rationalizations to sculpt. I contented myself with staring guiltily at the neglected tooth every time I brushed. I made apologies, and promised the tooth that I would get it the necessary attention once I moved on to real life.

Months later, I was in real life and it was not as advertised. I was jobless and had moved back in with my mother. Without the stress of thesis to distract me, I began to notice the aching more and more, to the point where it became inescapable. The hole in the tooth had gotten larger, and seemed to be a functioning repository for all my guilt and angst over my present condition. Through a friend of a friend, I managed to get a free consultation with a dentist who laid out my options. The tooth would be all right for a couple of months, but at some point would just crack in half. The dentist described this possible event as the most painful thing I could imagine, on par with giving birth through my eye socket, and I took him at his word. I described my whole employment situation, and he told me what I already knew: "If you think that you're going to get a job in the next few months, we can let it go. If you think there's a chance that you might not find work, you have to address it."

Thinking for a second, I opted for the latter.

"What can I do to address it?" I asked.

He answered, "You can get a root canal and a crown that will be about $3,000. Or we can just pull it, and that will be $225."

This was not the first time that I thought seriously about value and architecture, but it did cast my meditations in a different light. I understood, in that moment, what a recession really was: it was the difference between getting a tooth fixed and getting it pulled. Pulling teeth, after all, was for poor people. Both my parents had grown up dirt poor, and had, as a matter of course, their own sets of falsies. These weren't teeth that had succumbed to age—they were the legacy of childhood poverty. What's more, my parents had worked their whole lives to make sure I didn't grow up that way. To accord me the benefits of the middle class, and the modern miracle of dental care. For all the time they worked, and the insurance they paid for, I was up shit creek.

I didn't have $3,000. I didn't have $225 either, but my mother was willing to loan it to me. I grudgingly decided to have the tooth removed. It was a difficult thing to get my brain around. I had given my whole adult life to architecture. Upon exiting graduate school, I was in six-figure debt. I had given countless sleepless nights to architecture. I had given my health, my youth, and too many relationships. And now, I had to give a tooth? Really? To something that's not giving back? It was like going back to that ex.

My lowest point, however, was still to come. The $225 covered a local injection of Novocain, but not general anesthetic. I tossed it around in my head for a minute, whether or not to spend the extra $100 on some ether. I decided against it. It was, after all, a time of sacrifice for all of us, so I would do my part to put up with a little pain, and save the $100 for something more important than my comfort.

The Novocain did numb my jaw, or most of it, but the removal of the tooth was one of the more traumatic moments of my life. The sound of my molar cracking in half was like hearing ceramic break. It was low and coming from inside my head—a place that did not usually generate that kind of noise. It was as alien to me as if I had heard a bird squawking from inside my chest. As I heard the pieces clink into a metallic tray like punctuation, I reorganized some priorities.

It was, for me, a rare moment of bitterness. It was a moment when I thought to myself, "This is what architecture is worth." It was also a moment of profound regret. I regretted skimping on the painkillers—and vowed never to make that mistake again. I vowed never to skimp on dental care again; I don't think I made the wrong decision by having the tooth removed, but there is something unsettling any time a part of your body is removed. Even if it is just a tooth. It was one of those moments when we mentally realign what's valuable, what's important, and what's necessary.

As the tooth came out, so did my romantic notions about architecture and its possibilities. I had previously understood that architecture required some sacrifice—meaningful things usually do. But I had, up to that point, also romanticized those sacrifices. I had somehow believed that the sacrifices made me a more credible architect—they proved how much I loved architecture. The hole in my jaw and the holes in my shoes (both metaphorical and literal, at that point) somehow established my bona fides. To expect more from architecture would be to somehow dishonor its elusive nature. All my heroes had toiled in poverty and obscurity for years before they found their way, right? My present sacrifices would eventually be woven into my own narrative and would serve as testament to how powerful and lasting my love of architecture really was, right?

Over the next few days, through a haze of Vicodin and ice packs, I unpacked all those assumptions and threw them away. Forgiving architecture for my present indignities was not an act of love; if one really aspired to love architecture, challenging its value should be a constant occupation.

We should expect it to give as much to us as we do to it.

8 | The Value Architect

To empower ourselves, we must understand the true value of what we do. The first thing to understand is that cost is not determinative. Our hearts and minds do not seek "cheap," however often it appears that way. If twentieth century economics is to be believed, the autoworker who is buying a small bungalow and the tycoon who is buying a mansion operate with the same motive: they are both trying to get the most for the least. Their processes may have different outcomes, but in both cases they seek *high value*, not *low cost*. Therefore, the critical difference between the two is in how they assess value. Value is merely the difference between the perceived worth of something and its objective, listed cost. While modern economic theory describes variants and anomalies to this truth, it can be safely said that on the whole, in the long run, across wide samples, this is *true*. We make decisions based on value, not on cost.

For all its complexities, the basic value formula is simple:

Worth – Cost = Value

Consider the autoworker shopping for a house. The autoworker encounters two houses, side by side. They are in the same neighborhood, obviously, and are in the same condition. The house on the left is 25 percent larger. For some strange reason, both houses are selling for the same price A. The A in this case would vary widely according to neighborhood and geography, but let's call it $200,000. The autoworker might not need a big house—perhaps the house on the right is all that he needs, spatially. But should he buy it? Economics says no. The house on the left is the better deal because it is the greater worth at the same cost. Real estate agents determine the worth of a house, in part, by its square footage. If the house on the left is 25 percent larger, it could be sold for 25 percent more, all things being equal. Assuming we bought a house and wanted to sell it tomorrow, we could buy each house for the stated $200,000. But we could *sell* the house on the left for 25 percent more.

This follows our intuition. Even if we really, really wanted the house on the right, we could buy the house on the left for $200,000, sell it the next day for $250,000, and use the $50,000 profit as a down payment on the house on the right.

Conversely, what if our autoworker had to choose between two houses that were the same size? What if everything about the two houses was exactly the same, except the one on the right was cheaper? In this case, the autoworker would be a fool *not* to pick the house on the right. If the houses are the same, he will get much more "value" by selecting the house on the right. Again, this follows our intuition.

What is interesting about these value exercises is that they are completely cost-*independent*. That is, instead of an autoworker buying a $200,000 house, our example could have been about a tycoon buying a $3,000,000 house and the outcomes would have been the same. A different price range, but the mechanics of the decision making are identical: both the tycoon and the autoworker are trying to capture the most value that they can.

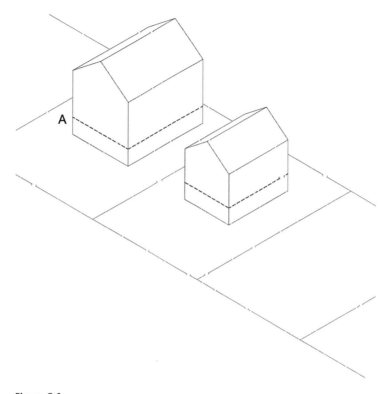

Figure 8.1
House value.

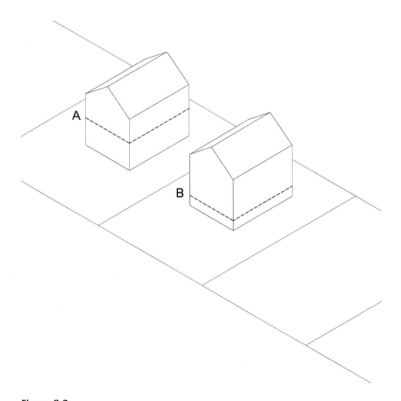

Figure 8.2
House value.

Our example was necessarily simplified. We would never find two houses that are exactly the same, because much of the worth of a house is tied up in the emotional and plastic experiences that it conveys. Houses cannot be appraised as objectively as we have done in our example. However, in whichever way one is inclined to measure worth in a house, the mechanics described remain true. Perhaps one person measures worth by how close the houses are to public transportation, another measures worth by critical merit, and a third by how much natural light the house gets. A fourth person measures worth by how pleasant the neighbors seem. Most people, when buying a house, measure worth by all of these factors in subjective ways that can be difficult to define. The point being that when it comes time to buy a house, we don't go out and look for the cheapest one. We don't even necessarily get the biggest and best one we can afford. Our decision making is *complex*. Likewise when we decide what car to buy, or where to go to college.

But for whatever reason, when we're looking at someone else's decision-making process, the temptation is to believe that they are simpletons, acting on the crudest impulses and merely trying to get the cheapest thing they can find. Especially when they're making decisions about architecture.

It is appropriate as a preliminary matter to challenge the idea that humans act rationally. The idea of rational actors is something that most economists and finance types would find oversimplifying and outdated. In the same way that the rules of architectural modernism have been unraveling over the course of the last half-century, so too have the rules of classical economics. There are too many exceptions to rational actor theory. If human beings are so rational, why do one billion of us smoke, despite all the evidence of its harmful effects? Why does Certs have Retsyn, or why do poor people play the lottery? There are plenty of examples like these.

Since we are not economists, there is no need to unravel this mystery. We must merely ask ourselves whether the decisions we make about *architecture* are rational. When someone buys a house, is he or she making a rational decision? When an architectural jury chooses Adjaye over Predock, is *their* decision rational?

We can qualify architectural decisions from other decisions in two ways:

• They will always have some component of subjectivity, and
• They will always be of a certain scale.

Architectural decisions will involve some component of subjectivity. They may be passionate, and there may be qualities that we can't fully explain, but they are nonetheless deliberate. There is a temptation to attach the word "irrational" to every decision that involves factors we can't articulate or quantify. We're deciding between two homes and somehow, subconsciously, one reminds us fondly of the house we grew up in. These memories weigh on our decision in a way that we can't or don't articulate, and they affect our choice. Despite the fuzzy nature of this reasoning, there are still options being *weighed,* and the decision is in that respect rational.

We can further make the case that architectural decisions are rational because of their scale. We *invest* ourselves in architectural decisions because buildings, even bad ones, are expensive. It is difficult to imagine anyone buying a building on a whim— we don't buy a building the way we buy useless bric-a-brac in the checkout line at the grocery store. We think about it. We fuss about it. Decisions about architecture are frequently made by committee, or by jury, or as a family, or as a couple.

When we describe value decisions in this book, we assume a certain amount of "rationality" on the part of the actors. We define that term perhaps differently than some economists, because we are only interested in it as it applies to architecture. A choice between Le Corbusier and Gropius need not follow any algorithm or science—it may come down to a feeling, and that is in that nature of what we do. It is based on *something* and is therefore not irrational or arbitrary.

Here we offer another important definition: the "worth" of something is not necessarily quantifiable, but this doesn't mean that we shouldn't be attempting to understand it. Any buyer of design or construction will have many criteria that together create some estimation of worth. For most architectural consumers, this will involve a balance of economic and noneconomic criteria. For an architect, it is the noneconomic criteria that represent the source of our insight and form the basis of our training—we culture ourselves to understand the experience of space rather than its profitability. We relegate the consideration of economic criteria to those other "lesser" professions, the only exception being the "cost" with which we are so frequently preoccupied. We should ask ourselves under what circumstances we would seek to expand our sphere of influence, and what could justify such an expansion. Architects long for it, because every architect wants to be a shaper. Each architect wants to have an effect on the physical world—from the aspiring starchitect to the selfless humanitarian. We cannot do this on our own, however; we need the cooperation of clients and other parties. We therefore seek to understand how these other parties make assessments of worth.

Worth is an extremely difficult economic concept to pin down. It represents what we *think* we are getting when we buy something. "Worth" is the sense that we got a good deal.

Suppose we are in the market for a home. We find the one we like and are scheming about what to offer the owner. We think the house may be worth $400,000, which, coincidentally, is the most that we can afford. We decide to offer $350,000, and to our great surprise the owner agrees! The owner doesn't even want to bargain. This is a great turn of events because we capture $50,000 in value that we didn't have to pay for.

$400,000	–	$350,000	=	$50,000
Worth	–	*Cost*	=	*Value*

Now consider an alternate scenario: we find the same house and make the same assessment—the house is worth $400,000. We bribe the real estate agent to spy on the owner, and find out that $400,000 is the lowest the owner is willing to go. We're still okay with the situation—we'll get a $400,000 house for $400,000. We won't get any free equity, but we found our dream house and are happy with the outcome. Now imagine a third scenario where we find the same house, make the same $400,000 assessment, but the owner refuses to go below $425,000. We immediately scoff. We are indignant! How dare this owner try to take advantage of us by thinking we would be foolish enough to pay $425,000 for a house that's only worth $400,000!

Reliably, we are excited by the prospect of a high-value deal. We will tolerate a zero-value (or break-even) deal. Deals that represent a value loss, however, we will not tolerate. Most of the time, they will anger us. For what economists call "value loss" we have many names: getting ripped off, being taken, swindled, etc. When we find out that something is worth a lot less than we paid for it, we call it a "lemon" or even "fraud."

We should acknowledge the rarity of such transactions. Anecdotally, frauds and lemons happen all the time, but compared to positive-value transactions that occur every day, they are actually quite rare. This is because our brains prevent us from engaging in negative-value transactions. Our brains *refuse* to let us pay more for something than what we think it's worth. Such a thing would have a *negative* value. Occasionally we get swindled, but the world economy marches forward because, on balance, people are pretty good at making the right decisions.

How might this change the way we think about cost? By telling us that cost is *only* important in its relation to worth. Returning to our house-seeking couple, is there a way that we can imagine getting them to spend much more than they can afford, merely by changing the worth in relation to the cost? Let's present them with two choices, using all the same assumptions. They have found their dream house, it is worth $400,000, and the owner has accepted their offer of $350,000. Is there a way to make them abandon their dream house and spend more than they can afford? Let's say that in the next neighborhood over, there's another house being offered. This house is appraised at $3,000,000, but the owner is willing to accept $800,000. $800,000 is *twice* the maximum that the house-seeking couple has said they can afford. But look at the value equation:

$$\frac{\$3,000,000 \quad - \quad \$800,000 \quad = \quad \$2,200,000}{Worth \qquad - \qquad Cost \qquad = \qquad Value}$$

We get $2,200,000 in value. At this point, the couple should be asking whether this is more house than they need, or whether they can afford the property tax on the house, or where the extra $400,000 is going to come from. But the smart economic decision is to buy the $3,000,000 house immediately. They should leverage everything they can, and get some co-signers. Why? Because they can turn around and sell the house the next day for $3,000,000.

That leaves our happy couple with a $2,200,000 windfall:

$3,000,000	–	$800,000	=	$2,200,000
Cash from sale	–	*Pay off mortgage*	=	*Windfall*

With the $2,200,000, they can turn around and buy their original $400,000 dream house, flat out. And still have $1,800,000 lying around to set up a retirement fund, or a college fund for their kids, or a down payment on an architectural education, should one of their kids decide to go that route.

It is difficult to imagine this scenario transpiring in real life, mainly because $3,000,000 houses usually don't sell for $800,000. We set out to prove, though, that we could make the couple *not* buy their original $400,000 dream house, and instead spend much more than they could afford on something else. How did we do it? Merely by altering the value involved. We raised the cost—doubled it, in fact—but we raised the *worth* by a factor of 7.5, and so the big house in the other neighborhood became the much more attractive option.

Every practicing architect has been asked to reduce costs. We can now understand this request as not, inherently, a request to reduce costs, but a request to increase or preserve value. When we start thinking in terms of value instead of costs, the nature of such requests starts to have logical roots. Suppose a developer is doing a $10,000,000 project. The developer calculates that after all the design, construction, and consultancy costs have been tallied, the total cost on the project will be $9,500,000. So the developer has $500,000 as his profit, for himself and his employees over the course of this project, which might take three years:

$10,000,000	–	$9,500,000	=	$500,000
Worth	–	*Cost*	=	*Value*

When we typically talk about a $10,000,000 job, we, as architects, assume this to mean "how much the project costs."

However, here we use it to mean "how much the job is worth." That is, if you sold the project the day after the ribbon cutting, how much could you get for it? Here, $10,000,000.

Let's assume a cost breakdown like the following:

Table 8.1
Cost Breakdown

Item	Cost
Site acquisition	$3,000,000
Consultants	$1,000,000
Design fees	$360,000
Construction	$5,140,000
Total	$9,500,000

For clarity's sake, we have excluded many of the costs that would typically be associated with a project like this. Now let's assume that our costs have started to climb. What is happening to the value of the project? Let's first consider a 5 percent increase in design fees:

$$\frac{\$360,000 \quad * \quad 5\% \quad = \quad \$18,000}{Design\ fee \quad * \quad Increase \quad = \quad Value\ loss}$$

The developer's value is reduced by this amount—it cuts into his or her profit. So the developer's new value is:

$$\frac{\$500,000 \quad - \quad \$18,000 \quad = \quad \$482,000}{Original\ value \quad - \quad Decrease \quad = \quad Diminished\ value}$$

This represents a 3.6 percent reduction in the developer's profit. Not an insignificant sum, to be sure, but not the end of the world either. Now, what if we consider a 5 percent increase in construction costs?

$5,140,000	*	5%	=	$257,000
Construction costs	*	Increase	=	Value loss

Conducting the same analysis:

$500,000	–	$257,000	=	$243,000
Original value	–	Decrease	=	Diminished value

The $257,000 loss represents a 51.4 percent reduction in the developer's profit! With a relatively small (5 percent) increase in construction costs, we have wiped out more than half of what the project was worth to the developer. That's why a 10 percent post-bid additional services fee may be negotiated, sometimes even amicably, but a 10 percent increase in construction costs will typically land someone in court.

However, the point of our analysis is not to sympathize with the developer, but to explore the idea of value. Let us now suppose again that we increase construction costs by 5 percent. We charge no fee for the extra design work, but there were certain changes that we, as professionals, felt we should see. Along with the 5 percent increase in construction costs ($257,000), imagine we have some way to demonstrate that we have increased the project *worth* by 5 percent. Let's conduct the same analysis.

$10,000,000	*	5%	=	$500,000
Project worth	*	Increase	=	Increase in worth

As a developer, my overall costs have increased:

$9,500,000	+	$257,000	=	$9,757,000
Original project cost	+	Increase in construction costs	=	New project cost

But my overall project *worth* has also increased:

$10,000,000	+	$500,000	=	$10,500,000
Total project worth	+	Increase in worth	=	New project worth

So what is the increased project value, in the developer's eyes? We return to our value equation:

$10,500,000	–	$9,757,000	=	$743,000
New worth	–	*New cost*	=	*Developer's new value*

This represents a 48.5 percent *increase* in the value, as perceived by the developer. We have created something that is 1½ times more attractive to the developer, and we did so *while* raising costs.

The difficulty in this sort of scenario is the actual quantification of the worth. How do we make a project that is *worth* more; and once we have, how do we go about documenting that increase? Quantification is a difficult, subjective task, but it nonetheless goes on every day. At some point, the developer in the aforementioned example sat down and determined that the project was *worth* $10,000,000, and this wasn't a guess. It was the result of measured analysis, market research, economic modeling, and risk analysis.

Should architects engage in such activities? Is that really how we want to spend our time? For the average architect, the answer would be a resounding "No." Moreover, architects typically aren't trained to perform these analyses in the way that professional market analysts and finance types are. However, the gist of the analysis is simple: value, not cost, is the driving principle behind economic decision making. We need to embrace the idea that value will always trump cost, and that by positioning ourselves as *creators* of value, we free ourselves from the tyranny of the cut-cost mantra. We need to find better ways to articulate and define the value of architecture, so that when we undertake a particular design strategy, we can confidently declare that it is more valuable than the alternative.

I fundamentally believe that good architecture is worth more, singly and collectively, than bad architecture. I would guess that most of my readers would share such a sentiment. But there are many throughout our society who do not. Worse still, there are many more who don't make a distinction between good architecture, bad architecture, and no architecture. Collectively, we need to make the case that good architecture is worth more, and that any architecture is a better value than no architecture.

My grandfather was not a learned man—not in the formal sense. But he had that earthy wisdom that comes from hard farm life, the wisdom that comes from living through the entire twentieth century, from living long enough to see the passing of most of his friends, his spouse, and his way of life. He had the comforting, easygoing nature of a man at peace, and although he could rarely remember my name (he would usually call me "Dennis," a reference to my older cousin), he was always willing to tussle my hair and impart a nugget of wisdom, which would unfortunately take me twenty years to decipher.

As can happen in modern families, my grandfather and I were separated not just by years but by cultures. The farm life that he had lived was as alien to me as any foreign country—his anecdotes irrelevant to my modern, Nintendo-obsessed life. It is also unfortunate that we often fail to understand the people in our life until they're gone, and understand the lessons they tried to teach us even later than that.

In my own case, my grandfather taught me how to make decisions when I was about five or six. He taught me to be perceptive, bold, and resolute. I listened to none of it. My time with my grandfather was usually spent searching his house for secret stashes of candy, and I couldn't be bothered to listen.

Well after his passing, I started to decipher Grandpa's lessons—one of them, anyway. I don't recall the context, but I remember him once asking me, with half a smile, "You know the difference between a horse apple and a cow pie, dontcha?" I didn't. Cow pie I thought I could basically understand; they would occasionally serve chicken pot pies in school, and I assumed a cow pie was something similar. Horse apple had me stumped.

As I grew into his knowledge, I started to get it. I started to wonder whether Grandpa had been trying to teach me something deeper about choice and resolution. Ninth grade biology class helped. A cow pie is a piece of cow feces. Cows eat grass, and because the cow is a ruminant, the grass is digested multiple times in a series of stomachs and what is excreted is usually mushy, stinky, and altogether unpleasant. A horse also eats grass, but because it is a nonruminant, it digests the grass much differently. The grass passes through the horse's system quickly and barely digested, relative to the cow. So what the horse excretes is still feces, but it's mostly grass, maybe some dirt. It is dry and hard, and roughly the same size as an apple. Hence the term "horse apple."

I like to think that what my grandfather was getting at was that cow pies are significantly more disgusting than horse apples. While they may both be feces, if you had to pick one, you would be less miserable settling for the horse apple. If confronted with such a choice, you shouldn't spend a lot of time bemoaning your fate or weighing your options—one is clearly better. Just dig in.

I think my grandfather was also trying to prepare me for the reality that sometimes life asks you to eat shit. And smile about it. The man had faced choices that would be unthinkable to someone of my generation—and yet seemingly remained clear about the difference between bad choices and worse ones.

The choices we face as professionals, and as human beings, are usually not as awful as that between a horse apple and a cow pie. But they are usually not that clear, either. We face no certainties in choosing one way or the other. And our choices are rarely binary—they get more multifaceted every day. With this infinitely expanding menu of choices, and the accompanying complexity of all of our options, the analysis and risk can be paralyzing.

Wherever there is risk, we can find reward. Such is the wealth that defined the boom leading up to the Great Wake. The workings of our contemporary financial system fundamentally concern the ability to ameliorate risk. If risk can be eliminated (at least on paper), then it makes sense to bet the farm. Which we did. When the financial rewards of betting the farm begin to cloud our judgment in the analysis of the risks, then we should begin to worry.

Architects should study risk—not because they want to be rich, but because risk is the great undercurrent of our culture. It defines how people make decisions, about architecture and everything else, and so it should concern us.

If architecture is seen as having a risk disproportionate to its value, then people will not want it. Risk is not a binary thing; we cannot classify things as "risky" or "safe," because those terms only really have meaning in relation to other things. We can, however, understand our design choices as "riskier" or "safer" than alternatives. We can imbue that understanding with our existing knowledge about design, cost, assembly, etc. and make better decisions about what to design.

DECISION MAKING

10 | The Risk Architect

Understanding how much something costs is easy; determining a level of riskiness is difficult. It is the science of making the right choices. In our daily lives, we rarely make efforts to quantify risk. We think about it, and have an intuitive understanding of the riskiness of different events, but make no special effort to attach numbers to it. As we recover from the economic crisis, we will face greater and greater incentives to monitor and control the risks associated with our design decisions.

Suppose our favorite band has just released a new album. Our favorite band is fairly consistent, but only one in three songs is actually one we would pay for. We consider buying their new album on CD, but we shudder at the thought of paying $15.00 and then finding out that the B side is loaded down with mediocre songs. We decide to buy their lead single on iTunes for $0.99 instead. We get one song for a dollar, instead of twenty songs for $15.00. On a per-song basis, iTunes is the more expensive decision, but nonetheless a better one because of the aforementioned risks. We can sample each song and only buy the ones we like.

What exactly is the risk of the album being a dud? Suppose there are 20 songs on the album and the chance of any one song being good is 33 percent. The formula for figuring out the likelihood of good songs on the album is given by something called the binomial distribution.[1] Using that formula, we can populate the likelihood of having x number of good songs on a twenty-song album:

Table 10.1
The Chance of a Good Song

At least this many good songs	Likelihood
1	>99%
2	>99%
3	98%
4	94%
5	84%
6	69%
7	51%
8	33%
9	18%
10	9%
11	3%
12	1%
13	<1%
14	<1%
15	<1%
16	<1%
17	<1%
18	<1%
19	<1%
20	<1%

Odds are pretty good that there is at least one good song on the album: 99.966 percent. The odds are also good that there are multiple good songs on the album: there's approximately a 51 percent chance that there are at least seven good songs on the album. But the problem of buying an album remains: if there is *only* one good song, you have essentially paid $15.00 for that one song. If there are two good songs, then your cost per song drops to $7.50. If there are three good songs, your price per song has dropped to $5.00, and so on, and so forth. So at what point does the cost of buying the album equal the cost of buying the songs on iTunes? In a riskless universe, when there are 15 good songs on the album. If there are 15 good songs, then we've essentially paid $15.00 for 15 songs, or $1.00 per song. The chance of that occurring is roughly 1/10,000th of 1 percent—not very good odds at all. Empirically, we know that if this were the whole story, no one would ever buy albums—everyone would get their music exclusively from iTunes and other online services.

To further uncover the mechanics of our buying decision, we turn to the concept of *expected value*. Expected value is merely the value of a certain event multiplied by the likelihood of that event coming true. We learned in chapter 8 that value is merely the worth of something minus its cost, so we can predict the expected value of something as follows:

(Worth × Probability) – Cost = Value

A good song is worth a lot to us. We can listen to it over and over, and it will reliably pick us up, or settle us down, or set a mood, etc. To keep the math simple, let's say that a good song is worth $5.00, and that a bad song is worth $0.00. Keeping in mind that only one song in three is going to be a good one, we can determine the expected value of a good song as:

($5.00 × 33%) – $1.00 = $0.67

Since a purchase would run the risk of the song being a dud, we can consider the expected value of a bad song in the same way:

($0.00 × 67%) − $1.00 = −$1.00

Adding the two results together yields an expected value of *negative* 33 cents. Therefore, this doesn't seem like something we would buy. Intuitively, this seems to fit: if we knew that we had a one in three chance of getting a good song, and we had to buy songs on an individual basis, we probably wouldn't buy this single. However, such mechanics are circumvented by iTunes, because it affords the user an opportunity to sample songs before purchase. With iTunes, you can be 100 percent sure that you're going to like the song, so your formula would look like:

($5.00 × 100%) − $1.00 = $4.00

We have made a convincing case for iTunes, but none of what we have discussed so far explains why albums still exist. While many people get most of their music through online sources, people still buy albums as well. Buying an album merely requires a broader application of the risks we analyzed above. Since the cost of the album is always $15.00, regardless of how many good songs are on it, we can fill out a chart of expected values like so:

Table 10.2

The Cost of a Bad Song

Number of Good Songs	Likelihood	Cost of Album	Expected Worth	Expected Value
1	>99%	$15.00	$5.00	−$10.00
2	>99%	$15.00	$9.96	−$5.04
3	98%	$15.00	$14.72	−$0.28
4	94%	$15.00	$18.72	$3.72
5	84%	$15.00	$21.03	$6.03

Table 10.2   (continued)

Number of Good Songs	Likelihood	Cost of Album	Expected Worth	Expected Value
6	69%	$15.00	$20.75	$5.75
7	51%	$15.00	$17.78	$2.78
8	33%	$15.00	$13.07	–$1.93
9	18%	$15.00	$8.18	–$6.82
10	9%	$15.00	$4.33	–$10.67
11	3%	$15.00	$1.92	$13.08
12	1%	$15.00	$0.71	–$14.29
13	<1%	$15.00	$0.22	–$14.78
14	<1%	$15.00	$0.05	–$14.95
15	<1%	$15.00	$0.01	–$14.99
16	<1%	$15.00	<$0.01	–$15.00
17	<1%	$15.00	<$0.01	–$15.00
18	<1%	$15.00	<$0.01	–$15.00
19	<1%	$15.00	<$0.01	–$15.00
20	<1%	$15.00	<$0.01	–$15.00

In almost all cases, the expected value of buying the album is negative—hence no purchase. If there are only going to be a few (three or fewer) good songs on the album, our purchase will not generate enough worth to justify its cost. The possibility that there are a lot (eight or more) good songs on the album is so remote that the expected value is similarly negative. There is a "sweet spot" of four to seven songs where buying the album makes sense, but other than that, we're inclined to buy the songs through iTunes.

Unless you are an economist or in marketing, you probably don't consciously work through this sort of decision making. But we still work through these decisions subconsciously—and

Apple studies them quite closely. That's why they invented iTunes, and that's why iTunes has been so successful.

Are there similar lessons for architecture? Certainly. Buying a building is significantly more risky than buying a disappointing CD. Most of us will never have to contend with the former. But risk is one of the factors that loom large—larger, certainly, than cost. This certainly seems counterintuitive. We have been told for generations by the developers and municipalities for whom we work that cost is paramount. It seems at every turn that we're being told to keep costs down. How can we easily envision a scenario where risk trumps cost?

Imagine that we take a trip to Las Vegas, and there are only two games in town. Both are Texas Hold 'Em No Limit Poker— one with a $2,000 buy-in and a $100,000 pot, the other with a $1,000,000 buy-in and a $10,000,000 pot. I'm assuming that very few of my readers could afford a $1,000,000 buy-in. I'm also assuming that most of my readers could raise $2,000, if they were sufficiently motivated. If my readers had to choose, they would choose the first game.

But now suppose we alter the riskiness of the two games— specifically, we fix the $10,000,000 game. God, Yahweh, Mohammed, and Robert Moses all swear up and down that they have the game fixed for us, and all we have to do is come up with the $1,000,000 buy-in. What is the smart decision then?

With no risk involved, the smart decision is to mortgage your house, your parents' house, and borrow from every aunt, uncle, and friend you know until you come up with $1,000,000. Collect the money and then pay everyone back the next day. You're up $9,000,000. By altering the risk characteristics of a situation, we have turned something that is profoundly unaffordable into the *only* option that makes sense.

We don't always have the luxury of divine assistance, so how might the issue of risk be relevant for a client and his or her architect? Let's imagine a project that might confront any one of us. This project will cost $7.5 million to execute, and after completion the owner will charge $65,817.87 a month in rent. The number is not rounded because this problem has been structured to have an internal rate of return of exactly 10 percent. "Internal rate of return" is a finance term, and you don't necessarily need to understand what it is in order to understand that higher is better.

In considering our project in a perfect world, there would be no risks of any kind; in our hypothetical universe, however, we're going to consider the risk of a delayed opening. Similar to what we did with iTunes, we can do a quick analysis of the delays, and the risk-adjusted costs of those delays:

Table 10.3

The Risk of Delay

Months of delay	Likelihood	Risk-adjusted cost in lost rent
1	50%	$32,908.93
2	40%	$26,327.15
3	30%	$19,745.36
4	15%	$9,872.68
5	0%	$0.0

In order to understand how this financially affects our project, we can recalculate the internal rate of return. I've omitted the actual calculation to avoid boring the reader, but the new internal rate of return dropped to 9.863 percent. In a nonperfect world, our project is predictably less profitable.

Can we envision a scenario in which we can get the client to pay more, just by diminishing the risk? Let's add $50,000 in construction costs, for a total of $7,550,000, but let's change the risk profile to the following and reevaluate the risk-adjusted cost of delay:

Table 10.4
Reduced Risk

Months of delay	Likelihood	Risk-adjusted cost in lost rent
1	15%	$9,872.68
2	10%	$6,581.79
3	5%	$3,290.89
4	4%	$2,632.71
5	3%	$1,974.54

It is telling that in this reduced-risk scenario, the internal rate of return is 9.88 percent. This is perhaps a small difference, but the point remains that we were able to raise the cost of the project and *still* make it more economically attractive. All we had to do was lower the risk, similar to the way in which we manipulated the two Vegas poker games.

At this time it is also worth examining risk as perceived by different players within the built environment. Architects and their clients are subject to very different types of risk—principally because the architect's success is bound up in the quality of the *design,* and the client's success is bound up in the quality of the *building.* The two *can* be extricated from one another. Because of the way we have structured our profession, we have created *asymmetries* of risk—that is, an activity that is enormously risky to nonarchitects is safe for architects, and vice versa. It can often be to an architect's financial and critical advantage to *increase* the risk endured by others. Consider the following two flow charts describing a client/architect interaction. The first identifies the client's positive outcomes, the second identifies the architect's positive outcomes.

Although certain contingencies have been removed from both for clarity's sake, we can understand these flow charts as describing the process of a design through various stages of competition, design, and construction. The first characteristic to observe is the cyclical nature of the process. That is, upon failure of the design process, the whole process resets. The client and (potentially) the architect go "back to the drawing board," as it were.

We should also note that there is a smaller loop embedded within the process: the back-and-forth between the client and the designer. The design will not move forward without approval of the client, but the designer may also opt out of the process at various points, if the designer feels that his or her ideas are not being allowed to develop, or if the client is being too overbearing, or for a number of other reasons. Both parties have an interest in seeing the design develop into a building; therefore both parties have an interest in negotiating. If they can, together, draw out of the schematic design a solution that is satisfactory to both, they both win big. However, what occurs in circumstances where the client and architect come to an impasse? Who wins and who loses, and what is being lost and gained?

For the client, what is most notable is that both positive outcomes are predicated by the completion of a *building*. The client has no inherent interest in design. That is, the client draws no ultimate gain out of the design process. The client may have gotten a good design, and may have paid fair value for it, but ultimately that is not the client's aim. With extremely rare exceptions, clients are clients because they are interested in buildings.

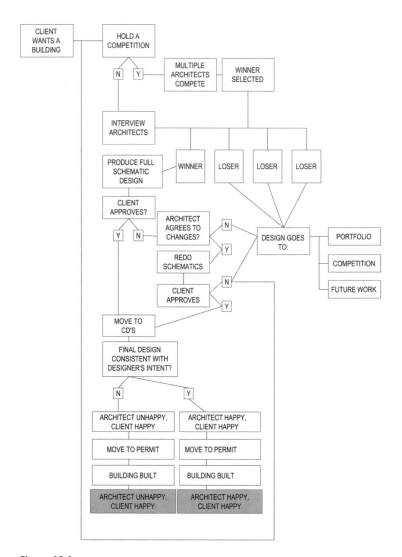

Figure 10.1
Client's outcomes.

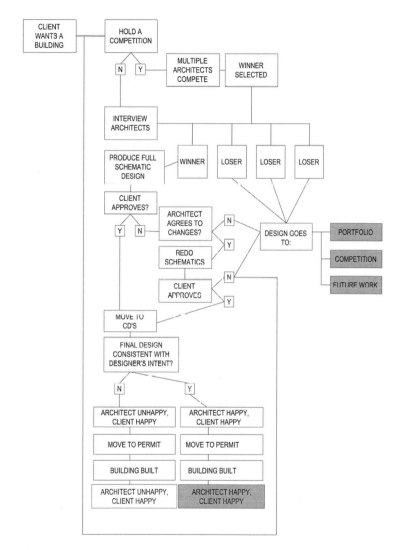

Figure 10.2
Architect's outcomes.

Whether the ultimate building is something satisfactory to the architect is not determinative in these diagrams. We make the assumption that the client is happy either way, because it is unlikely that a building will be fully executed if the client is unhappy with the design.

The second diagram shows the positive outcomes for the architect. What is notable here is that the architect has multiple avenues for a successful outcome. Clearly, the architect is most successful when the building is fully executed according to his or her design. That is the outcome that architects spend their whole lives pursuing. However, there are other positive outcomes even where the design does not get executed. The designer may add the design to his or her portfolio, and incorporate it into a body of work. The designer may enter it into an unbuilt design competition, and, assuming a victory, receive all the press and distinction that comes with this. The designer may just use the completed design in other ways to achieve future work in the same field. This isn't to say that an architect is pleased when a design is rejected by the client, but we must clearly understand that rejection by a client is not always the end of the road for a designer. Indeed, sometimes sticking to your guns may prove better, professionally speaking. If the client is demanding changes that would be received poorly in critical circles, the architect may wisely decline to make such changes, and save his critical reputation in the process. The architect, at least among her peers, is now understood as a woman of integrity.

The asymmetry of risk may or may not alarm an architect. To some architects, it would seem normal that their interests and risks, and those of their clients, diverge. Every architect knows at least one client with whom this divergence seems, in retrospect, to have been as inevitable as it was justifiable. But what happens when *the entire profession* is positioned in this way? What happens when our *collective* risk profiles become not only misaligned with but *opposed to* the world that pays our fees? Architecture is deemed too risky   it is set aside.

Riskiness is rarely positioned as a design consideration. Architects understand the risk of finding clay in the soil report, or a bad slump test, but when deciding between wood studs and metal, we rarely seek to quantify the risk involved in the choice and, more importantly, to weigh the risk against the relative costs involved. To be empowered, we must begin to do so. The Great Wake is about risk. Everyone from the Treasury Secretary on down made some poor estimations of riskiness; we will certainly think differently in the future. Our design decisions will be even more reliant on how risky or stable something is judged to be, rather than how much it costs.

11 | I'm an Architect

During my professional years, the worst part of my day was always the tie. It didn't matter how badly a project was going, or what I was working on—the tie was always the worst. It never made sense to me. I began each day by tying a useless scrap of cloth around my neck. In a knot. I might as well have started the day by chaining a rock to my ankle or using Tabasco as aftershave. At some level, I understood the concept of fashion—I understood that the tie was some sort of inheritor of the cravat, which was some sort of scarf. At some point it was used to ward off consumption, or catch food stains, or something else that would have been a big deal in Victorian Europe. I understood that as an architect, it was my privilege to indulge in a bow tie—a fashion choice that many architects adopted because normal ties would interfere with hand-drafting. However, I never did any hand-drafting. Wearing a bow tie, therefore, seemed to make even less sense than wearing a regular tie. A cravat would have raised too many questions, and not wearing a tie never seemed to be an option at any of the firms I worked at. My tie options seemed limited. Along the way the tie has evolved, getting narrower, in every sense of the word. As much as I tried to be useful in my day and in my work, I began every day with the ultimate symbol of futility.

I never got used to it. Its regularity did not make it easier or less frustrating. I learned to surmount the dread and self-loathing that accompanied every morning tie—that is, I could get over it and get on with my day. The act itself, however, was never any less revolting. Some days, it was worse than others: the days I wore an ugly tie. Occasionally, the laws of tie rotation would require me to wear one that was out of date, or that I was sick of, and the day would be a little worse for the fact that not only was I wearing a useless scrap of cloth around my neck, I was wearing an ugly useless scrap of cloth around my neck. Even among the bad days, there are worse days.

In my postgraduate wanderings, one such worse day occurred as I applied to work at a temp agency. The Great Wake had taken me under. There were no architecture jobs to speak of, and I had reached a point of desperation. Although I had few preconceptions about the world of temping, and the temps I knew seemed like decent, hardworking people, temping nonetheless seemed like a step down. I felt in some way that I was acknowledging the invalidity of all the skills I had spent the last ten years building. There was a cold, late spring rain on the day that I went to the temp agency, and the brief walk from the Metro station to the temp office took me past the office building where my father used to work. Its earthen brick stood out against the usual colors of the downtown Washington palette, and if you're ever in town, it's an easy landmark. My father made sure that I understood it as a waypoint, so that if I were ever lost downtown, I would be able to find him. I cruised past it, however, more concerned about the beating rain and a battered umbrella that would have been replaced months ago if not for the unemployment I was trying to combat. It shielded me on the way to the temp agency, and I stayed its commitment to the scrap bin. We were both refugees, my umbrella and I.

Everything about the process felt like a poignant criticism. The employee who received me and processed my application was nice enough. After I told her that I was an architect she asked if I had any office experience. I didn't exactly know what the question meant—after a moment of pause I concluded that she was asking whether I could tie a tie and file papers and copy things and what not. I answered, "Yes." She took out a heavy ballpoint pen, and while I was busy filling out tax forms and releases, she proceeded to mark up my resume. She excised the section detailing my awards and honors. She excised the section describing my volunteer work on the Katrina reconstruction, my nationally regarded references. She didn't get into it, but she didn't have to. None of these things were important to the people that she would be showing the resume to. The people who would be ringing her phone simply didn't care—therefore, neither did she.

None of the employers that might call upon this particular temp agency were interested in an architect or his design abilities. They wanted someone who could copy things without jamming the machine, who would show up to work sober and not rob the place at lunchtime. I was all of these things, and it seemed that these qualities were, in the middle of 2009, more marketable than being an architect.

I know she didn't mean it to be the final indignity, but she asked me to sign a form acknowledging that I would submit to a drug test. I was tempted to say something snarky like "Which drugs would I get to test?" and thought for a minute about expounding on Coleridge and Freud and S. Thompson and all my other heroes who carved truth and progress out of 26 letters, 10 digits, and a few grams of whatever was lying around. Instead I just signed the form. She asked me a few brief questions in what must have passed for an interview there—read off a Xeroxed form with palpable disinterest. She seemed relieved when she got to the last one: "What do you think sets you apart from other candidates applying for this job?"

"I'm an architect," I answered, and dated my signature.

12 | The Paid Architect

Although my temping experience cast doubt on my value as an architect, I remained convinced that architecture as an activity actually had an assessable value. Assessing the economic value of an enterprise is straightforward. you merely have to ask, "How much is someone paying me to do this?" The question isn't a personal one. The question is not whether any particular designer is being paid, or whether any particular design contract is a profitable one. The question is whether design, as an activity, pays.

A simplistic answer might point to architects and iPhone designers and fashion designers and say yes, of course design pays—these people have jobs. People shell out big bucks for iPhones and Prada—enough to give us confidence in the market value of design.

The clear truth is that people are paying. But what exactly are they paying for?

In the fields of marketing and product development, it is customary to break down the price of a product or service and determine how much of the purchase price is going to what. For many decades, marketers worked to segment the public into different kinds of consumers, so that mail and television advertisements could be more targeted; this segmentation is adequately discussed in *The Harvard Guide to Shopping* and we will not be delving into it here.

Newer methods, however, focus on the segmentation of actual *motive*. When we begin to understand the component parts of motive, it not only helps us in deciding how to advertise but in deciding *what to make*. Consumer products are in a state of constant, directed evolution, designed by scientists but inspired by your own desires. For instance, when a father is grocery shopping and buys a $5.00 box of cereal, the $5.00 may be allocated among the different priorities he may have. $2.50 may represent the base cost of cereal. That is, the father needs to buy cereal, and if he really didn't care what kind of cereal his family ate, $2.50 would be the cheapest he could get. The extra $2.50 he pays can be the result of several factors. Maybe $1.50 can be attributed to his kids screaming. He's walking down the aisle and his kids start screaming about how they can't *possibly* eat a cereal that doesn't come with a toy, and for the sake of peace and expediency the father relents. However, there are several cereals with toys, and he's willing to pony up a little extra for something that comes with a toy and is also healthy. So he bends a little further and goes for the $5.00 cereal. His value breakdown would look like this:

Table 12.1
Buying Cereal (Normal)

Value	Motivation
$2.50	Base cost
$1.50	Makes the kids happy
$1.00	Peace of mind gained by knowing the cereal is healthy
$5.00	**Total**

By compartmentalizing the motivations, those who make and sell cereal can focus their resources differently. Imagine this scenario:

Table 12.2
Buying Cereal (Pushover Dad)

Value	Motivation
$2.50	Base cost
$2.50	Makes the kids happy
$0.00	Peace of mind gained by knowing the cereal is healthy
$5.00	**Total**

How is this customer different? He doesn't care whether his cereal is healthy or not, but he's willing to pay a lot to keep the kids quiet. If you were in charge of designing this cereal, you would design it to be brightly colored and sugary. You might make sure that the cereal was placed down low—between the ground and 36 inches above the ground, so that kids walking past with their parents will be sure to see your cereal and start screaming. And then the opposite case:

Table 12.3
Buying Cereal (Healthy Dad)

Value	Motivation
$2.50	Base cost
$0.00	Makes the kids happy
$2.50	Peace of mind gained by knowing the cereal is healthy
$5.00	**Total**

In this case, the father is seemingly immune to his kids' screaming. The only thing he cares about is getting something healthy for them, no matter how unhappy it makes them. If you were in charge of designing this cereal, you wouldn't necessarily make it brightly colored—in fact, you would be indifferent to the color, because the father is indifferent on that point. You would be sure that the cereal is on a shelf between 44 and 76 inches above the ground (the perfect sight angle for adult males), and make the box fairly neutrally colored. Thus, we have three different fathers, each paying the same amount for the same amount of cereal. And yet it is possible that they buy very different cereals (like fathers 2 and 3) or can choose either (like father 1).

We might run the same analysis on design activities. When someone shells out $600 for an iPhone, are they paying for the sleek black casing? The ease of use? The functionality? Are they paying that much because they are sheep and *have* to have the latest gadget?

Some combination, certainly, and everyone's combination would be different. But we know that someone at Apple is studying this very, very closely. Let's investigate a hypothetical example: an individual buys an iPhone for $600, and the sum of that cost can be allocated to different motivations.

Table 12.4
iPhone Value Breakdown *A*

Value	Motivation
$50	Need phone
$100	Need MP3 player
$150	Need PDA
$100	Convenience of having them together
$35	Like all the cool plug-ins
$65	Like how it looks
$40	Enjoy the attention
$60	Buzz—the excitement and peer pressure built at the point of iPhone's release
$600	**Total**

Which of these different payments are related to design? Some of them seem to be more technological achievements than design ones. The phone and the PDA are nothing really special. Even having them in one device is not new or inventive. The cool plug-ins are an interesting designed quality, but again seem more like engineering and software design than the Design that an architect might be more familiar with.

The buzz is a good *marketing* design. Steve Jobs does a brilliant job of creating the "next best thing," and nurtures the idea that anyone who doesn't have an iPhone is some sort of Luddite. In fact, Apple has always been successful at branding itself as the company of the young, the professional, and the technologically sophisticated—and at painting its rivals as the company of their parents (Apple's 1984 "Revolution" commercial springs to mind).

The only buyer's motivation that would fall into the traditional purview of a Designer seems to be "Like how it looks." This doesn't mean that "design" is "that which is superficially attractive." Where the iPhone is concerned, a closer definition might be "able to do all the other stuff, but looks cool at the same time." Not a perfect definition, but one that deductively fits, given that designers seem to coo over the iPhone but not over the Samsung Omnia, which is functionally similar.

Is that what people are paying for? The ability to achieve aesthetic excellence *beyond* just plain technical excellence? According to all my architect friends, the answer is yes. Unequivocally yes. The reason the iPhone is successful is because it *looks* sexy. To them, the customer is responding this way:

Table 12.5
iPhone Value Breakdown *B*

Value	Motivation
$50	Need phone
$100	Need MP3 player
$100	Need PDA
$50	Convenience of having them together
$20	Like all the cool plug-ins
$200	Like how it looks
$20	Enjoy the attention
$60	Buzz—the excitement and peer pressure built at the point of iPhone's release
$600	**Total**

If that's true, then you ought to be able to produce a device that has all the functional assets of the iPhone, wrap it in an ugly exterior, and still sell it for $400. Similarly, you could take a device that is supremely *dysfunctional* and has none of the bells and whistles that the iPhone does, sex it up, and still sell it for a couple of hundred dollars. An idea that seems borne out by the following comparison:

Table 12.6
Phone Comparison

	Samsung Omnia	iPhone	BlackBerry Storm
Price	$269.99	$600.00	$249.99
Contract	2-year contract	2-year contract	2-year contract
Fixed memory	8 Gb	8Gb	1 Gb
Variable Memory	HotSwap 16Gb SanDisk	None	HotSwap 16Gb SanDisk
Weight	4.34 oz.	4.76 oz	5.47 oz.
Talk time	346 minutes	480 minutes	270 minutes
Display	3.20-inch color	3.5-inch color	3.25-inch color
Camera	5.0 megapixel	2 megapixel	3.2 megapixel
MMS	Yes	No	Yes

If you only read the top line, the case might be closed. The iPhone is at least $300 more expensive than the other two phones. Even the fact that the three look more or less the same does not bring them into the same price range. Clearly, people are paying so much more because the iPhone is so sexy! Well, maybe not.

Remembering our cereal example, we can look to the different component parts of the three phones and ask what, exactly, is being paid for. We would have to conclude that in many respects the iPhone is a better phone, regardless of what it looks like. It has a longer talk time, a bigger display, and greater onboard memory. Could it be these features that people are paying for, at least in part?

Something else about the iPhone makes it interesting to study. After only two months on the market, the 8Gb model was dropped in price from $600 to $400, strongly suggesting that a great deal of the phone's value was tied up in buzz. The iPhone had just come out and everyone *had* to have one. Therefore, the following might be a more accurate model:

Table 12.7
iPhone: Understanding Buzz

Value	Motivation
$50	Need phone
$100	Need MP3 player
$100	Need PDA
$50	Convenience of having them together
$20	Like all the cool plug-ins
$60	Like how it looks
$20	Enjoy the attention
$200	Buzz—the excitement and peer pressure built at the point of iPhone's release
$600	**Total**

If you take away the buzz, then, you have a phone that is only worth $360. The $100 or so premium that people are paying for the iPhone over the Samsung Omnia or the BlackBerry Storm could be attributable to the "design" or just as well to the other advantages that the iPhone brings (greater talk time, larger screen, etc.).

Professional product developers have means of uncovering how all these numbers break down. The process basically works like a tickle test. They tickle one part of the body and see how much the subject laughs. Then they move on to another part of the body. Through a process of trial and error and linear regression, they eventually discern what the most ticklish part of the body is. Similarly, they can discern the most important component part of the purchase price—that is, what people are paying *most* for.

Can a similar analysis be done for architecture? When a city or a developer or a company or an individual pays an architect for his or her service, what exactly are they paying for? Momentarily setting aside the fact that an architect's involvement is statutorily required in most cases, what can we say about what is "valuable" and what is not? We'll begin with a crude breakdown; let's assume a $20,000,000 job where the architect is paid a 7 percent fee, or $1,400,000.

Table 12.8
Breaking Down Architectural Services

Value	Component
$200,000	Schematic design
$900,000	DD and CD phases
$300,000	Construction phase
$1,400,000	**Total**

We call this a crude example because it only identifies the phases that an architect works in. It's an example that most of us are used to seeing—we tend to submit fee proposals in this way. But it doesn't reflect what is actually being valued. It also suggests that there is something universal about these phases. How can we begin to think differently about pricing in a way that might illuminate more clearly *why* we get paid?

Suppose that instead of an "ordinary" architect, we went out and got a high profile, award-winning designer to do the initial design. We then hired another, less well known architect to execute the bulk of the work. We would have to pay more for our high-profile designer, so our breakdown might look like this:

Table 12.9
Payment for Good Design

Value	Component
$400,000	Schematic design
$900,000	DD and CD phases
$300,000	Construction phase
$1,600,000	**Total**

People don't pay for services—they pay for the value those services create. The fact that an architect wakes up every day and puts pen to paper is no guarantee of employment, as many architects can attest. So what is it about these services that is creating value? We can break the services down in the same way we deconstructed the iPhone. Maybe this is a better way to think about it:

Table 12.10
Architectural Services: Nuts and Bolts

Value	Phase	Component
$200,000	*Schematic design*	*Base cost*
$100,000	Schematic design	Buzz/marketing
$100,000	Schematic design	Need good "paper" to convince the investors that this is a good venture
$600,000	*DD and CD*	*Base cost*
$150,000	DD and CD	Firm's reliability
$150,000	DD and CD	Easy working relationship
$200,000	*Construction*	*Base cost*
$50,000	Construction	Firm's reputation for integrity
$25,000	Construction	Don't yet know who contractor is going to be
$25,000	Construction	I can handle the contractor, but having the architect by my side during punch list meetings will be pretty valuable
$1,600,000	**Total**	

Using this hypothetical, we can start to make an assessment about the value of design. We should remember that these numbers represent *value,* not cost. This isn't what the architect gets paid, this is what the services are *worth* to the client. We must also consider that there are both direct and indirect relationships to design. A well-designed building will probably run more smoothly during the construction phase. An *elaborately* designed building may proceed more slowly, out of necessity. Either way, there may be a significant relationship between these different components of the worth.

What can be said about those components that deal most directly with design? Among these we can certainly include "Buzz/marketing" and "Need good 'paper' to convince . . ." The rest of the components don't appear to deal *directly* with design: we can easily imagine a firm that is great with design and terrible at all these other components. Most of us can probably name a few, right off the top of our heads. Most of us probably also know a few architects who are exceptional with all the non-design-related components, but mundane when it comes to their designs. What is critical is that we understand *how* our clients are making these payment decisions. In the case of the high-profile designer hypothesized above, the client is paying an extra $200,000 for the services of a high-profile as opposed to just an "ordinary" architect—in fact *twice* what they ordinarily would for schematic design services. If $200,000 represents the "base cost"—the minimum that one could expect to pay for schematic design services, if only cost mattered—then the $400,000 that this client paid represents a 100 percent increase. Such a scenario would make a pretty convincing case for the value of good design.

Now consider an alternate example: a high-profile designer whose revolutionary design creates nightmares throughout the CD and construction phases. Let's assume that the client is still willing to pay for good design, to the tune of $400,000. But because the high-profile designer in this example is difficult to work with, the services of "firm reliability," "easy working relationship," and "I can handle the contractor" are severely devalued. Remember that these numbers are what the architect is *worth* to the client.

Table 12.11
Valuing Services

Value	Phase	Component
$200,000	*Schematic*	*Base cost*
$100,000	Schematic	Buzz/marketing
$100,000	Schematic	Need good "paper" to convince the investors that this is a good venture
$600,000	*DD and CD*	*Base cost*
$50,000	DD and CD	Firm's reliability
$60,000	DD and CD	Easy working relationship
$200,000	*Construction*	*Base cost*
$50,000	Construction	Firm's reputation for integrity
$25,000	Construction	Don't yet know who contractor is going to be
$15,000	Construction	I can handle the contractor, but having the architect by my side during punch list meetings will be pretty valuable
$1,400,000	**Total**	

In this case, we have a client that appreciates good design *and* is willing to pay for it. But because of the other price components, the overall value is the same as it was with the "ordinary" architect.

All of these examples are speculative. They are not meant to be declarative or to make a case for either "ordinary" architecture or starchitecture, merely to illustrate that the valuing of services is a nuanced matter. While we understand "design" as the core of what we do—our most valuable act—we should understand that it is not the only activity within the professional purview of an architect. The increased value provided by good design can easily be offset by the derivative effects of that same design or designer. Understanding the value of design as positioned against other services is crucial.

We must understand our value—and structure our fees—based on client perception, rather than phases and hours. If we find that, on balance, clients *don't* pay for design (for our architectural ideas), we should be alarmed. If we find that, even where our top designers are involved, clients *still* aren't paying for design, we should panic.

I had a minor existential crisis when I first heard about the pet rock. I was twelve or so and saw one for sale at a garage sale. I asked the lady what it was, and she told me: "It's a pet rock."

I asked what it did and the nice lady replied, "Oh, you know, it's a . . . pet . . . you dress it, and talk to it . . . and . . ."

I interrupted: "It's . . . a . . . rock."

The lady and I stared at each other the way two people do when they don't speak each other's languages and pantomime isn't working. The bun in her hair told me she was a straight shooter, but something told me she was pulling my leg. That were I to purchase this rock, I would somehow be playing the fool on a stage I could not see. I stared for a few seconds, awaiting clarification; I got only a pursed smile. I left empty-handed.

The whole thing bothered me on my way home. I oscillated between feeling like a fool and feeling like the smartest person in the world. Was it really possible to glue eyes on stuff and sell it as pets? That didn't seem right. But if it was, I would have a few ideas. I could glue. And I had enough allowance to buy more than a few googly eyes.

My father had never been one for pop culture fads and didn't seem to have any idea what I was talking about, even though he had lived through this phenomenon. I turned to the encyclopedia (the

old-fashioned Internet), which gave a brief description of the phenomenon but not so much of why it caught on. Why did millions of people
all of a sudden decide they would adopt rocks as pets?

I have believed ever since that pet rocks were the greatest dumb idea
in history. I was raised by a couple of secular humanists and was always
led to believe that in a free market, money flows to good ideas. If you
have a good product or service, it stands to reason that, all things being
equal, someone will want to pay you for that product or service. If you
have a really good idea, then people will want to invest in it, because
they will want to partake of the future success that will surely be yours.
How, then, do we explain the pet rock? The pet rock fad was started
by an advertising executive named Gary Dahl. The premise was simple:
take ordinary rocks, glue eyes on them, and market them as pets. This is
a colossally stupid idea. If I were a bank and someone walked through
my door and requested a business loan to start a pet rock business, I
would probably call the police. Nonetheless, the idea attracted money
(from somewhere) and managed to make Dahl a millionaire. In the
most basic sense, Dahl made value, and it made him money.

The corollary to this is that if someone is not paying money for your
ideas, then your ideas are not good enough. By implication, if you enter
a competition along with 199 other entrants and do not win, you have
not created any economic value. Your idea might have been good, it
just wasn't the best, as judged by the jury. No one is going to pay you
for that idea. In strict economic terms, the work that you did is worth
less than the pet rock.

We all know this to be a silly conclusion. Of course the work we did
has some value, even if it didn't win the competition. It has value to us,
because we learned something. Maybe we now have something that
can go in our portfolio and can be used to our future advantage. But
the fact remains that we came up with an idea, it was good, and we
didn't get paid for it. Sometimes, our best ideas don't earn us a dollar.

14 | The Idea Architect

As we struggle to understand new ways for architecture to create value in society, we have to be mindful that we're creating value for architects as well. Architects do not always attract the financial rewards of other professional services. For the amount of training that we go through, we earn quite little, despite the fact that income is typically correlated with high education, prestige, and other dimensions of professionalism.[1] Architects, it could be argued, chase other motivations. We don't work for money so much as for truth, justice, and the American way. We work for beauty, or glory, but never for profit! Luckily, this book is not about how to make profits, but it is about how to empower design amid the Great Wake, and for that reason we should look to evolutions in our profession that will not *decrease* our own economic security. We must understand that creating value and protecting it can be two separate things. We already know that our ideas are valuable. How do we make sure this translates into value for us as professionals?

First and foremost, we stop giving value away:

> Developers and clients with continuous building in programs have grown to accept that architects, in their enthusiasm to get "their" design built, will often give away, for little or no fee,

their high-value advice on framing the brief and conceptual design.[2]

Second, we understand that while the most valuable aspect of our enterprise may be design, there are other services to which the architect is predisposed which are considered high-value in their own right:

> It is ironic that today the high-value services are increasingly provided outside the core of the design and construction process, at the pre-project and post-project stages. These services—master planning and estate strategies, strategic briefing, option appraisal and ongoing facilities management—are well suited to the architect's expertise and are valued highly by the client in achieving business success.[3]

Third, and most importantly, we understand that relinquishing control over those *other* services does not necessarily mean that we get more control over design processes or are able to perform them better:

> The architect has been much diminished in the now centuries-old splintering and segregation of the former role of the master builder. Ironically, by narrowing its realm of significant interest to appearance only, architecture has sacrificed control of its one remaining stronghold: appearance.[4]

There are many ways to create value as an architect. What is astonishing is how readily the profession passes over most of them. Our roles as master builder and client's representative were not wrested from us in some Machiavellian scheme—we gave them away. It was easy, since most architects would much rather be designing than doing title checks or verifying lien waivers. It is a plain fact that much of what made the professional service of architecture valuable has eroded, and less clear whether those skill sets can be brought back in the house of architecture.

In this chapter, however, we will examine the architect's main means of creating value: through design; through ideas.

Basic rules of patent and trademark suggest that when you come up with a good idea, you become valuable. This is at the heart of capitalism, democracy, and modern progress. Sometimes, as in the case of the pet rock, even when you come up with a supremely dumb idea, you also become valuable. Modern laws of copyright, patent, and trademark exist to protect innovation at all levels. This does not mean that innovation exists for the sole benefit of the innovator. Most patents exist for a limited time period—so that the benefits derived from the innovation will eventually be generically available. Abstractly, an innovator wants his or her innovation to be dispersed. An author wants to be read. Inventors want their inventions to be used. A musician wants his or her music to be heard. Our copyright and patent laws exist to create a balance in some way: they seek to allow innovation to be dispersed and create benefits both for the innovator and for those who would utilize the innovation.

As architects, innovation is at the core of what we do. However, we are different from other creative industries in that we operate as a professional service—that is, the fruits of our innovation effectively become property of our clients. In the purest legal sense, architectural designs are typically "instruments of service" and are retained as property of the architect. However, the long-lasting benefits of our ideas do not flow back to us in the way that royalties flow back to an inventor, because while we may retain intellectual property rights, designing buildings is essentially a one-off service. To design responsibly, we have to begin each new project in an earnest effort to find something new. We don't necessarily seek newness for its own sake, but any design task begins with a unique site, at a unique point in time, and good design therefore requires a unique solution. We can't, in good conscience, take a design for one client and slap it onto another's project. We may successfully capture the intellectual property rights associated with a particular design (of little use once the building has been executed), but all the other benefits are captured by others.

Unlike musicians, artists, authors, inventors, and other innovators, architects often seem ready to give their ideas away. These other innovators go to great lengths to *protect* their work. They copyright, they patent, and they trademark. As a professional culture, architects don't protect their ideas very well.

Whatever the mechanics of professional service law and intellectual property, of much more interest here are the *cultural* reasons that architects often give their work away. The origins of this culture are known to any architect.

Architecture school is about creativity and innovation. Unlike many other academic programs, which reward the mastery of an existing body of knowledge, academic architecture rewards the ability to see problems in new and unconventional ways. It rewards, in theory, the creation of new ideas. Architecture students do not get paid for these efforts, however. They in fact pay enormous sums of money to come up with new ideas. Whatever a student creates during the course of his or her studies is then typically used as material for the portfolio. The student can claim creative credit for the work, and on the basis of that work may obtain employment and recognition. The intellectual property rights, however, remain with the school. An architect begins his or her career in a flurry of uncompensated ideas. Through sleepless nights in studio, far beyond the workload expected of any other area of academic study, architectural students compete to produce the best idea, and are cultured to believe that wide approval of the idea is the only compensation they should covet. Approval, as a form of compensation, is powerful enough to make architecture students forgo the normal aspects of academic life, such as periodic idleness, sleep, etc.

It could be argued that a student's ideas aren't robust enough or developed enough to merit compensation anyway. The cultural inheritance of an architect's academic life, however, sets the stage for a professional life that can be similarly unrewarding. Architects move into their professional lives *expecting* not to be compensated. We are taught that the ultimate reward for our efforts is to see our designs realized in built form. The disposition of that built form and its externalities become secondary. All future economic benefits of the building, beyond the initial design fee, are set out of reach. The future cash flows from rent or leasing, the appreciation in the equity, the resale value, etc. are all retained by the owner.

To some degree, this seems fair—the owner paid for the design, the construction, and the land. However, we can abstractly understand that a *good* design produces a *good* building, and that a *good* building is more valuable than a *bad* building. So who captures the benefits of the building, assuming that it turns out to be so good? What compensation is available for the good designer who produces the good design which produces the good building? A design is a professional service, but it is essentially an *idea* for a building. In other services and disciplines, when an innovator births an idea and that idea is realized in the form of some *thing*, the innovator takes some perpetual reward out of the realization of that idea. An author, an inventor, or a writer collects royalties. An architect does not, but more interestingly, the architect *does not expect to.*

Neither does the architect seem like other professional services on this point. Other professional services do not collect royalties per se, but there is at least some perpetual benefit derived from what they do. Other professional disciplines have some means of self-perpetuating. Better doctors mean we live longer. But living longer opens the door to more health problems, which means we need more doctors. Every time an attorney litigates a case or files a brief, it is added to the great body of common law, thus ensuring that greater numbers of attorneys will be needed in the future to sift through the common law that their antecedents made.

Architects are in an unfortunate place, deriving neither the benefits accorded to their fellow artists nor the self-perpetuation mechanisms secured by their fellow professionals. A client requests a certain building and perhaps provides a program. An architect designs a response to the design task and receives certain rewards. The architect receives a design fee, the publicity, the critical regard, perhaps a variety of emotional and psychic rewards, depending on how the design turns out. The architect, however, cannot use the design again. The recycling of old ideas is seen as the mark of an inferior architect.

Architects readily, and openly, give away their ideas. For the price of a 7 percent design fee, we readily hand over our best ideas. A compromise that is probably only tolerable because we have, from the beginning of our architectural training, been told that such a giveaway is normal. We live in an *idea* society and an *idea* economy. Architects cannot continue to give away their ideas if they seek to be an empowered and respected profession.

As meager as 7 percent sometimes is, architects often, in a variety of forms, give their work away for *free*. Broadly speaking, there are two distinct areas of free work: knowledge sharing and competitions.

Knowledge sharing can take many shapes, depending on the era and industry in question. In some respects, knowledge sharing is unavoidable in architecture. An architect designs a building, and that building exists as a statement for all future architects who come across it. Before the written word, the printing press, and the computer, architects found ways to share their knowledge with the world through built form.

The information age, however, redefines the act of knowledge sharing for all professions. For the first time in history, it is possible to share a discovery with the whole world, more or less instantaneously. For architects specifically, it is no longer necessary to build or publish in order to share one's ideas. We can quite literally sketch something on a cocktail napkin and make it available to the whole world within minutes.

Global, instantaneous knowledge sharing creates an unprecedented platform for innovation. It took mankind 500 years to get from the printing press to ENIAC, but only 50 years to get from ENIAC to the iPhone. This would seem to be good news for artists, inventors, and idea makers of all stripes. But for architects, who have the aforementioned tendency to give away their ideas, it creates opportunities to give away valuable ideas faster and more completely than ever before.

The accelerating pace of innovation has been dubiously named "viral" in the technology industry. It is the process by which particular ideas spread themselves throughout the network, constantly mutating and evolving. In one sense this is the way ideas have always spread, but in a wired world we can watch it happen with dizzying speed. In part this is due to how digital technology, in particular, is spread. Because digital technology is infinitely replicable, it can be passed from source to source without corruption. To the extent that a piece of digital output changes while being passed around, this arises out of some desire or deliberate action.

By way of contrast, consider the childhood game of "telephone" as applied to a new musical number. If a musician were to write a song and play it for a friend over the phone, the general melody and phrasing might remain intact, but certain notes would be lost. If that friend were then to play the song for a third friend over a different telephone line, a similar effect would be observed. A few notes gained, a few notes lost, and down the road we might have an entirely different song.

It would be quite a different thing to record that song digitally and send it to my friends as an MP3. The reproduction would be perfect. However far down the road it went, the song would be exactly the same. *Unless it were deliberately changed.* A friend might decide that the balance was off and adjust the bass and treble. Another friend might decide to add a few bars of improvised lyrics. My original song becomes an armature for innovation, and my friends and I, collectively, are tightly wound in a creative process. We are sharing our respective bodies of knowledge to create a song that no one of us, individually, could create. In such a situation, we should ask ourselves how the song's progenitor protects his or her original creation. Where music is concerned, it is merely through royalties. If I write and copyright a song, and someone else wants to make some changes to it and then profit from this new version, they are free to do so as long as I receive compensation. I can, at my liberty, grant certain individuals the right to use and modify the song however they want, free of charge. In sum, I can do whatever I want with the idea, because it is *my* idea. I own it.

Can architecture be transmitted in such viral ways? Can we send a design out into the ether where others tweak it in the pursuit of ever more beautiful forms and efficient methods? Can architects participate in a global knowledge factory and produce ideas that are better, faster, and more economically attractive?

To some degree it is already happening; internally this is how most firms already work. Architecture is and always has been much more collaborative than the public believes. Rather than sweeping this collaboration into the closet of necessary realities, viral advocates revel in its possibilities. They point to the Internet itself—arguably the best invention of modern times—which was invented by no one. And everyone. It is the result of billions of incalculable contributions. Can we follow IT's example?

Perhaps we could start by examining the differences between IT and architecture. While they are both "idea" fields, certain differences should be obvious from the start. Architecture has an artistic quality to speak of. While there are many IT professionals who would argue that programming is an art, there is a difference between art and Art. Then, architecture deals with formal and tectonic issues—in a very public way, no less. The training of an architect and a programmer are also quite different, and architects are subject to licensing and legal concerns that programmers avoid. It is simple enough to declare that computer programmers make more, on average, than architects. But considering how salaries scale can tell us much more about professional motivation.

It is possible to make a lot of money as an architect, as it is as a programmer. But architectural salaries scale more quickly. They start low and ramp upward. A first-year programmer makes an average of one-third more than a first-year architect—and no advanced degrees are required. Suffice it to say that architects have much greater incentives to move up the ladder than do programmers. Architects move up that ladder on the basis of their ideas. When they have good ideas or good designs, they get recognized internally or externally and move up. Architects can also get paid for their project management expertise, or their technical competence, but fundamentally what distinguishes an architect is his or her ideas. It is the architect as innovator that sets him apart from being merely technically proficient.

Intuition tells us something else: you can be a pretty average programmer and still make a living. You can traffic in the mundane and still support a family. In strict economic terms, going into IT makes more sense. Going into architecture doesn't make much sense at all—*unless* you expect to be successful. And unless you can bring good ideas to the table and take credit for them, it is difficult to imagine how you would be economically rewarded. The very mechanics of economic success within our profession run painfully north-south with the act of knowledge sharing.

Setting aside economics for a moment, we can turn our attention to the matter of critical success. To a nonarchitect, the pathways of critical success within architecture may seem straightforward: men of heroic genius rise to stardom behind inspiring works. To those within the profession, the paths to critical success are a little more intricate. Ostensibly they have to do with making good "design," but since that term is so hard to pin down, there must be more complicated mechanisms at work. For our purposes here we can make a simple observation: critically successful architecture is a very steep pyramid.

Every profession has a pyramid, whether steep or shallow. The steepness merely reflects the proportion of people at the top of the profession as compared to those at the middle and bottom. Professional sports, for instance, makes a very steep pyramid. There are thousands of young men and boys who aspire to

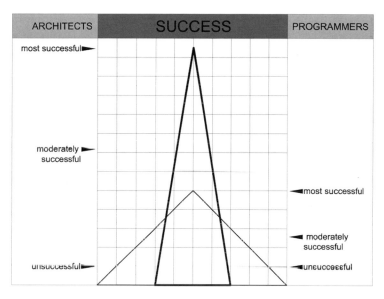

Figure 14.1
Two pyramids.

dominate the NBA. Unfortunately, you can be the best player in your high school and not get a college offer. You can be the best player in your college and never get drafted. You can make it to the NBA, but land on a doormat team. And at any point during this journey, you could tear an ACL and end up out of basketball forever. There are approximately 20,000 high schools in the United States; assuming that there are 5 basketball players from the senior class at each school, and that every one of them plays or practices 75 days a year for three hours a day, 22,500,000 hours are spent each year by these young men preparing for the NBA. Since only sixty players are selected in the NBA draft, only 0.06 percent of high school players ever have a chance to be economically rewarded for what they do. For those that can reach and persevere at the top, the rewards are great. But for those in the middle, or those at the bottom, the rewards are nearly nonexistent. A similar phenomenon can be observed in the field of acting, or of being a fighter pilot. There are so few available spots at the top, and the rewards are so great, and the aspirants so many, that the mechanics of the profession take on a certain curve.

It is perhaps because of this curve that we have come to institutionalize design competitions as another form of free work. We have come to accept them as the means by which we can vault ourselves from the bottom of the pyramid straight to the top. Design competitions deserve special consideration when we contemplate knowledge sharing. They are innovation buckshot. The architectural community throws a lot of pies at the fence, and hopefully one of them sticks.

The basic structure is simple. The client publicizes the event, attracts a small group of architects and stakeholders to serve as jury, and after varying amounts of procedure and/or hullabaloo, publicly proclaims the winner. Some competitions are relatively

fast and informal—and may not ever be known to those outside the profession. Others are very public and hotly debated,
such as the competition for the World Trade Center site in Lower
Manhattan. Some get built. Some just get published. Whatever
the case, competitions have grown increasingly popular as a
stand-in for a traditional schematic design phase. They are perceived by many to be a more democratic way of deciding our
collective architectural fate. A young, unknown aspirant can
take the architectural world by storm, as did Maya Lin with her
design for the Vietnam War Memorial in 1981, at the age of
21. The influence of old, dated architects is marginalized (or at
least tempered) and architectural progress marches on, at least
in theory. Since the Chicago Tribune competition in 1922, competitions have also been seen as a way to discuss and navigate
emerging ideas in architecture. The Chicago Tribune competition itself was notable for bringing out the best and most excit-
ing modernist proposals, although the eventual winner was a
Gothicized historic tower by John Mead Howells and Raymond
Hood. Architects study the losers of this competition more than
the winner; any first year lecture on architectural history and
the competition will show entries of Adolf Loos, Walter Gropius,
and Bruno Taut, despite the fact that none of the three earned
even an honorable mention.

It has, however, been a while since the Chicago Tribune
tower, and we don't so much discuss the losers of our present-
day competitions. Occasionally we discuss the second or third
place finishers, but otherwise the entrants fall into obscurity. Architectural competitions, like aspirations to be in the NBA or to
become an astronaut, are only really rewarding for the winners.

Consider a hypothetical architectural competition. This competition is for a $20,000,000 job and has 200 entrants. The en-
trants spend an average of 360 man-hours on their entries—the

equivalent of three people working for three weeks. All architects in this scenario are billing at $100 per hour. Therefore, each entrant can be expected to spend $36,000 in preparing a proposal, on average. The winner gets a $50,000 prize, the runner-up $25,000, and the third place finisher $10,000. The winner will get the design contract, and a fee equal to 7 percent of the construction costs. The first, second, and third place finishers also get *publicity*. A very difficult thing to quantify monetarily, but let's say, at a minimum, that it results in more work of a similar size at some point in the future. The first place finisher might get two similar jobs out of the publicity, the second place finisher might get one, and the third place finisher might get the equivalent of one-half a job. Critical success can't necessarily be measured in this way, but in the absence of better yardsticks, we will use it as a proxy.

Table 14.1
Competition Costs

	1st place	2nd place	3rd place	4th–200th
Expense of proposal	−$36,000	−$36,000	−$36,000	−$7,092,000
Prize money	$50,000	$25,000	$10,000	$0
Design fees	$1,400,000	$0	$0	$0
Publicity	$2,800,000	$1,400,000	$700,000	$0
Total	**$4,214,000**	**$1,389,000**	**$674,000**	**−$7,092,000**

As we can see, the top three finishers finish ahead, economically. The second and third place finishers are in a positive position assuming that the competition does lead to future work; the winner of the competition is ahead either way. She gets the prize, the fee, the acclaim, and the future work. She is the Kobe Bryant of architecture.

This accords well with our conventional notions of architecture, merit, and success. She *won* the competition, and therefore is entitled to all the trappings of fame and fortune. Her entry was deemed to be the best, by an impartial "blind" jury of architectural experts. So where is the problem? We have to look at two parties: the owner and the profession as a whole.

The owner who organized the competition does not owe anything to the losers of the competition. The owner only wants to deal with the winner. Even the second and third place finishers aren't coming over for dinner. In many competitions, the second and third place finishers don't even get a prize. Despite this, the owner gets an enormous pool of talent and body of work. The owner is the recipient of $7,200,000 in schematic design services, for which he only has to pay $85,000 in fees. The owner can cherry-pick the entries that interest him, and send the rest away. The owner can even elect to throw *all* the solutions in the trash and proceed with a cheaper alternative. In a noncompetition situation, the owner might still pay the same $85,000 for schematic design services, but instead of having 200 architects working on the problem, he would only have one. The owner is in a position to mine the best ideas of our whole profession, and only has to pay for a fraction of what's been produced.

And what of the profession as a whole? In this particular example, the profession ends up in economic *loss*. We establish this by totaling the gains and losses of all four columns:

Table 14.2
Competition Costs, by Profession

	1st place	2nd place	3rd place	4th–200th
Total by entrant	$4,214,000	$1,389,000	$674,000	−$7,092,000
Total for profession	−$815,000			

The economic value of the effort that the losing architects put in is greater than the economic *gain* afforded the winners, by over $800,000. One might suggest that this is only a concern to the losers. But what we are witnessing is a developer or municipality or corporation and indeed society itself devaluing our services. In economic terms, society is saying that the benefits of design are worth less than what they cost to make. Assuming the architects in our example are billing at $100 per hour, the architectural community has put in *72,000* hours into the schematic design phase, generating ideas and designs for the client's project. Another 14,000 hours in the contract phase. And through all of it, the client only pays a total of $1,485,000, for an average hourly rate of $17.27. As an industry, we're getting paid one-sixth of what we're worth.

Architects are notorious for devaluing themselves. They often find nobility in long hours and low pay. It becomes part of the mythos: the starving artist, the genius, the noble sacrificer. An architect forgoes the material comforts afforded to the lawyer or the doctor because it's the noblest thing to do when one is in the service of beauty. The difficulty with this sort of thinking is that it ignores a fundamental reality: what we do is valuable, and we're only getting paid one-sixth of what it's worth. We have allowed our profession to be structured in such a way that we almost have to lose, in a way not dissimilar from nineteenth-century medicine when a few prominent doctors jostled for the business of a few affluent invalids, while the rest of the medical profession "risked becoming a cut-throat, cut-price trade."[5]

To save medicine from being a cut-price trade, visionary doctors worked to establish the superiority and legitimacy of *every* doctor, not just the ones who could attract or find themselves affluent clients. The medical profession acknowledged that some doctors were better than others, but made the case that *every* doctor was a serious professional providing a valuable service. This transferred influence and prestige from the individual practitioner to a professional structure from which all doctors could benefit. Obviously, architects lack such a beneficial professional structure, despite the efforts of the AIA. Our professional structure is much more like that of acting than that of medicine. For any architect who reaches the apex of the profession, the rewards are immense—and go far beyond the monetary. For those who do not reach the upper levels of their profession, what other rewards are available for their ideas? Ask your closest architect. Certainly you will get different answers—and they will largely have to do with how happy that architect is with his or her work. That work will derive some mixture of economic, emotional, and critical rewards. Often we trade one for the other. Where none are present, we should consider our ideas wasted.

For these reasons we must remain skeptical of competitions, or anything else that devalues our work, in whole or in part. We must take full advantage of technical knowledge sharing and grow through its possibilities. But at the same time we must be mindful that technology always has the potential to rob us of ourselves. It enables us—but it also enables those who would devalue what we do. We must remember that a good idea will always be a valuable thing.

15 | The Basis of All Things

I was about eight when I fumbled my naiveté and accidentally took a few lurching steps into adulthood. I was in the backyard of my father's house, sitting in the branches of the knotted maple that rose out of the center of the yard. The maple was many things to me—a playground, a refuge, a source of intrigue and exploration. Between the ages of five and eight, the maple gave me many of my first scrapes and bruises—I learned how to climb by learning how to fall. I learned about bugs, gravity, and the seasons, all while sitting in the low broad branches of that tree.

On one particular day I learned about knowledge, and fear; the whole drama of human consciousness started to poke its way into my mind. Of course, at that age I lacked the cognition and vocabulary to completely understand or record these events, but I've tried to recreate them here in the spirit of the original episode.

I was sitting in the lowest branch of the tree, looking out onto the woods to the east. This wasn't unusual for me—as a child I was probably overintellectualizing and spent a tragic amount of time alone and staring off into space. Had I been born twenty years later, I probably would have been medicated. However, doping children had not yet come into fashion, so I was left to my own devices, as long as said devices were out of doors.

The woods were not deep or thick, but they hosted a menagerie which, at that age, still seemed expansive. I would walk through the woods and occasionally find a turtle, or snake, or rabbit track, and imagined myself a gentleman adventurer who was destined for fame within the pages of National Geographic. *On this day, however, the jungle came to me. Perched on my branch, I saw a white-tailed deer cautiously emerge from the brush, twisting its neck to better position its nose, trying to catch the scent of any possible predators. It paused at the brush line and looked both ways with obvious deliberation, like a new mother crossing the street. Its first few steps were tepid. Then, with more confidence, it strode out into the center of the yard. It was at this point that I realized it was headed for my father's garden, and the adolescent tomatoes that I would shortly be asked to cull, assuming the deer didn't get them first. It was the first time in my life that I had been that close to a deer—it was probably a good thirty or forty feet, but to my young mind it looked like I could reach out and grab it by its strong neck, swing myself around onto its back, and ride it off into the woods triumphant.*

White-tailed deer get their name because that's what you usually see. They're usually running away before you get a chance to get close, and the bob of the white fur on their tails is the extent of your contact. That was as much as I knew about deer, until that day. As the deer strode languidly beneath me, I saw its fine short fur, its lean musculature and obsidian eyes, scanning all around.

The most amazing thing to me was that the deer was not running away. It had no reason to—it couldn't see me. Or smell me, or hear me. Between my stillness and my elevated position downwind, I was completely invisible to the deer.

It is worth mentioning that, at this time, I found the woods behind my house terrifying. At night, I mean. At night there was a sea of blackness in those woods, and behind the brush line there were a million monsters, all scheming to find their way into our house. Even from the safety of a well-lit bedroom on the opposite side of the house, I would lie awake in worry. As if to torture myself, I would scurry downstairs in the middle of the night, look out the back door, and check to see if I could spot any monsters approaching. I never could, which of course just meant that their attack was imminent. The bugaboos that plagued my late evenings evolved as I grew, from shifty goblins to hockey-mask-wearing psychopaths to Amber alert felons. Fundamentally, though, they all emerged out of that blackness. They found their home in what I couldn't see.

Looking down upon the deer, I realized that that was the difference between us (the most important one, I mean). The deer couldn't sense me, and so was unafraid. I was specifically afraid of what my senses could not detect. In some eight-year-old way, I understood this as the burden of consciousness, and a condition unique to the human animal. I understood what William Faulkner meant when he declared that "the basis of all things is to be afraid," although I would not read those words for many years.

A lack of sensory input frightens humans. Contrastingly, animals do not feel fear unless it is supported by some sensory input—the smell of a predator, the rustle of grass. The absence of such input makes them feel at ease. I also realized at that time that imagination was the root cause of all of this. Human beings, unique among animals, could imagine what their senses told them was not there. An imagined thing could be as real as the tangible world, and would always extend out beyond the knowable. My imagination would always exceed what I was able to sense, and as such I would always be afraid. It was a terrible day in my eight-year-old world. I felt I had become a grown-up all at once. But in another way I realized that the course of life was to become a master of one's fears, to operate in a way that accommodates the unknowable, rather than becoming its prisoner.

I changed then. I tried to be okay with my lack of knowledge, and it set the tempo for many of the things I did up until architecture.

In confronting architecture, I had to evolve further, or de-evolve, depending on how you look at it. It is hard to say, "I don't know," either as an architect or an architecture student. It's hard to be okay in one's ignorance.

As a nine-year-old, I could look out into the black woods and say to myself, "It might be full of monsters, or it might be full of nothing, and I'm going to go to sleep either way." As a 25-year-old professional, however, it was difficult to say, "That ceiling could be 10 feet, or it could be 11 feet, and the building is going to be just fine either way." There is, as we will see, a pressure to be declarative. That in itself is hard because of the unknowns involved in the architect's work. We size rain leaders based on assumptions about the amount of rain a site will get, and we assume that the client will clean the gutters responsibly. But we can't write into our specs: "4 inch downspout, unless client is a flake, then make it 6 inches." We are asked, through a variety of phenomena, to know the future and other unknowable things. We are asked to represent ourselves in such ways. We are asked to review the facts and make convincing statements about what the rain leader needs to be. On the less technical side, we are asked to solve even more esoteric problems such as "What does a brick want to be?"

Most often, we capitulate to this demand. We make claims, and make them convincingly, over a field of doubts and a fury of our own insecurities. We do so because the task demands it. We convince ourselves that we see the whole picture, because it's hard to design around what you can't see.

16 | The Knowing Architect

To be empowered, we must understand the limits of our own vision. Architects are often called upon to learn a great deal about a subject very quickly, and in so doing can often come to believe that they "know" that subject. This tendency to overstretch has its roots both in their academic training and in the professional environment in which they operate.

In an academic setting, an architect student's semester is fairly routine: a professor selects a project or subject matter for the semester, and the student is expected to respond. The student begins with some period of research, investigating precedents, the site, and other aspects of the subject. At some point, a student is asked to "start designing," which can come in many forms. A student may start sketching, or building models, or just thinking and talking. This might be overly simplistic—in many ways designing and crafting is an act of research itself. But specific investigation into history, precedent, or operations can often be limited. A student may be asked to design a library during the course of the semester, and only devote a few weeks of that semester to researching the nature and history of libraries. The student is asked to represent a level of knowledge that rises far above what might be available to nonspecialists, despite having only briefly studied the matter. Because architectural study is about becoming an expert *designer* and not an expert librarian, shortfalls in that library knowledge are rarely caught, or acknowledged, or sanctioned. An architecture student's design may be faulted if it displays some obvious logical shortcoming (e.g., putting all the books on the ground floor when the library is sited in a floodplain), but an architecture student is not expected to display the nuanced judgment that a librarian might bring to the table.

Frequently, the student is not even required to confront the inconvenient. In designing his City for 3 Million Inhabitants, Le Corbusier famously described his process thus: "Proceeding in the manner of the investigator in his laboratory, I have avoided all special cases, and all that may be accidental, and I have assumed an ideal site to begin with."[1] It is questionable whether Le Corbusier had ever been in a laboratory. The average scientist would find such a proposition absurd. Scientific investigation does not begin by *avoiding* or ignoring special cases. Scientists may make efforts to exclude statistical outliers, or marginalize random events that might compromise the intent of the study. But such exclusions are done with rigor. These procedures are documented and repeatable. They are not used merely to exclude information or phenomena that the scientist finds inconvenient. The exclusions do not even rise to the level of personal choice or creative proclivity—they must be done such that another scientist, working elsewhere, would make the same exclusions.

However, Le Corbusier's method would probably not strike any architect as absurd. Most of us were schooled precisely in such methods—not necessarily by any one person, but certainly by the isolation of the design studio. A student's research can frequently operate in a closed loop created by the drawing board, the computer, architectural periodicals, and the Internet. Within this loop, the inconveniences associated with real-world practice are easily and enthusiastically discarded.[2]

Without having to worry about nettlesome zoning laws and dowdy historic review boards, our architecture student can get more in touch with the true purpose, meaning, aesthetic, ethos, spirit, etc. of a library. The absence of minutiae will likely never be an issue, for our architecture student is not judged or evaluated by a panel of librarians, but by a panel of architects. He or she is not required to be certain, or even necessarily to be right, so much as to be *convincing*. However, there is a flaw in this need to convince—the mirror deceives! An architecture student's incomplete idea becomes a beautiful rendering, and begins to deceive both the student and the critic, like a convenient lie told too many times.

As architecture students move into their professional years, they will certainly find themselves in front of a panel of librarians (or doctors, or executives, or whomever the client might be). At that time, however, other mechanisms will act to reinforce this false knowledge. If an architect is approached by a client who requests that the architect design a library, the architect has only one real answer: "Yes." Architects don't usually turn down work, for a variety of reasons which we won't delve into.

If an architect is approached with a project for a type of building he has never done before, it is seen as an opportunity to expand his portfolio. An opportunity to branch out. If the architect has never done a library, he has several options. He can go through a rapid research process and try to educate himself on the design and building of libraries. Or he can hire a new project manager or project architect or designer who has specific experience in designing libraries. One thing you will probably not hear the architect say is, "I'm not qualified to do that, maybe you should hire another architect."

Again, the architect finds herself in a familiar position: she has no expert knowledge of libraries, but she is expected to design anyway. She is expected to represent herself in a certain way: as someone who knows what she's doing. This is obviously a professionally dangerous and morally ambiguous place to be. The AIA's *Handbook of Professional Practice* advises that "it is a disadvantage for a firm to be known for too many things." A claim it supports by arguing that

> from a client's viewpoint, it is confusing enough to sort out the many competing firms, much less one firm with multiple messages. If your firm is known for restaurants, clients will assume you cannot possibly do a courthouse. If the client cannot figure out what a firm does, the client cannot select it.[3]

Clients seem to support this idea, if the market is to be believed. If a client is doing a stadium, they seek out a firm that has specific experience with stadiums. And the architectural profession has obliged them by becoming increasingly specialized—there are now firms that do exclusively stadiums, or laboratories, or schools, etc. While such a firm might not label itself as "expert" in stadiums, it can accurately represent that it has more experience and expertise in designing stadiums than any "normal" architect.

This market evolution raises the question of what it is that the architect is supposed to know: How to design? Or how to design something knowledge-specific?

When an architect is called upon to design a project, any project, he or she can bring to bear a number of different kinds of skills. Every architect brings something different, but we can roughly catalog these skills into three basic sets. We will call the first one "design skill," for lack of a better term. It encompasses whatever exists beyond the practical: the beautiful and the spiritual aspect of what we do. For the moment, we can think of it as whatever exists beyond the ability to merely fulfill the dry requirements of a program. Daniel Herman's definition of "high" architecture is useful here. In a footnote, he specifies "high architecture" as

> the realm of architectural discourse constituted by architecture schools, museums, journals, book publishers, the curators and the critics. It has its hotbeds (*El Croquis,* the CCA) and its perennials (Philip Johnson, the AA). It is anything found in a design library or bookstore. It is architecture that is reputable—and published.[4]

Herman's definition is problematic—primarily because it excludes the public *and* the client. Despite its elitist leanings, it is a workable definition for our purposes here.

The second skill set constitutes what we might call "general technical knowledge"—the technical knowledge that every architect is *supposed* to have. This general technical knowledge is obtained through the standardized processes of education, training, and licensing. Presumably, every architect, no matter what he or she is designing, is familiar with basic building codes and structural principles, for example.

The third component might be called "specialized technical knowledge" and pertains to specific project types. For instance, certain practices are niche practices and survive on one specific type of project, like laboratories. They market themselves as laboratory experts on the basis of the fact that they have done so many laboratories, or of how well they have done them.

Although the combination of these skill sets is not arithmetic, for diagramming purposes it will help to understand them this way:

$$\text{Design skill} + \text{General technical knowledge} + \text{Specialized technical knowledge} = \text{Finished design}$$

Over the last thirty years or so, the profession has undergone a segmentation of sorts. Encouraged by the AIA and helped along by market forces, we have developed a professional environment in which it is possible to do only two of these things and still obtain work. There are many firms out there that market themselves as pure designers—they don't pretend or admit that they have any specialized knowledge about a particular project type, but they make the case that they should be given the job because their design skills are so formidable that they transcend the expert knowledge offered by niche practitioners. An architect can practice like so:

$$\text{Design skill} + \text{General technical knowledge} = \text{Finished design}$$

Consider OMA's design of the Seattle Public Library. OMA likely did not campaign for the work on the basis of their having spent the last twenty years exclusively designing libraries, but on being expert designers. In doing so, they challenged the conventional understandings of what a library should be, even going so far as to propose hospital units for the homeless within the library—turning what was conventionally understood to be a nuisance into a design feature.

Unfortunately, OMA is more of an exception than a rule in this regard. Many more firms market themselves on the basis of their general technical knowledge or their specialized technical knowledge. Survey the Web sites or mission statements of any number of firms and you will be inundated by "We have X many licensed professionals" or "We deliver projects on time and on budget" or "We have over twenty years of experience in designing Y." What is professional about architecture has been elevated above what is artistic. Clients *want* to know that their architect is an "expert" in designing whatever it is that they're designing. They aren't trying to "reinvent" the library, they're just trying to do one very well in conventional ways. We'll describe one such firm (call it Firm X) as follows:

$$\text{General technical knowledge} + \text{Specialized technical knowledge} = \text{Finished design}$$

This isn't to say that Firm X isn't "designing"; they are, just not in the way that Herman defines it.

Thus, two very different kinds of knowledge can be the basis of a firm's success. The history of business, however, does not well agree with either OMA or Firm X. There is a place in history for companies and individuals who do one thing very well. They usually enjoy a certain amount of success, but soon falter. The fads change, and their products do not. Their competitors and imitators catch up, and it is soon difficult to understand what was so special about them in the first place. Companies that are successful in the long run share the quality of being able to create a valuable, interlocking network of skills and capabilities that is hard to replicate. In the same way that a stick-built house is very unstable until sheathing is put on, a business that consists of only one component will fall down eventually.

Such logic explains Google's growth into a contemporary behemoth. Google emerged in the late nineties as a search engine.

It was a quantum leap beyond previous search engines; in contrast to its predecessors, it would typically return results pertinent to one's search queries. It became a giant when it expanded into other, related sectors. It developed GMail and Google Maps, and bought Blogger and YouTube in an ongoing attempt to "catalog the world's information." What makes its strategy formidable is that all of its functions relate to one another. If I'm searching for a restaurant to celebrate my birthday, I can look up restaurants on Google Search. Google Maps can look up the address for me and give me directions. I can videotape the festivities, post the video on YouTube, and link to the video on my blog, so that those friends who couldn't attend can do so post facto.

The iPod—the ubiquitous symbol of hipness and technology—debuted in 2002, and Apple lost money that year. It wasn't until 2003, with the release of iTunes, that the device started to take off. Why? Because Steve Jobs engineered it such that iTunes could *only* be played on an iPod. As previously discussed, iTunes made a lot of sense for the consumer, not because it was necessarily cheaper than buying an album, but because it eliminated the risk of buying an album and having the B side loaded down with mediocre songs. The iPod appealed to consumers; iTunes did as well; but *together,* they became a juggernaut that captured an unheard-of 70 percent market share of all downloaded music.[5]

Such is the basis of all corporate strategy. By creating a web of skills and relationships, you create a business or industry model that is extremely difficult to duplicate. If you only have *one* skill, or have a series of skills that can easily be cleaved apart, you are vulnerable to competitors and imitators. It is the weaving that is the key.

How is this relevant for architecture? On the level of the firm, such history encourages us to diversify our skills and offerings. But in a profession-wide discussion, it encourages us to reevaluate what we find valuable about ourselves. We have organized ourselves into "design" firms, "niche" firms, "genius" firms, etc. According to basic business theory, however, we create value when we *synthesize* different offerings. That is, the best architect is one who has design skill, general technical knowledge, *and* specialized technical knowledge. A firm that is both a "genius" firm and a "niche" firm would be the best choice for any project. It is the binding of these skills together that makes them valuable. From a practical standpoint, this is hard to envision—no one can be an expert on everything and most firms are too small to maintain a competency across multiple project types. However, it is enough to begin now with the recognition that specialization is not necessarily a good thing. One thousand firms all picking out niches may add up to something very bad for the profession. Concluding that "design" or "project management" is our skill set is equally destructive when evaluated at a profession-wide level.

We must have some boundary around our own knowledge. But we can also think of new ways of designing that reinterpret our role as experts. We could define "expert" designer as someone who doesn't necessarily know everything about a particular project type or style, but can expertly design around the extent of what he can't see.

Recall the cautionary tale of the blind men and the elephant. Six blind men approach an elephant, feel around, and each comes to a different conclusion. The first man thinks it's a wall. The second man, grasping the tusk, thinks it's a spear. The third man grabs the trunk, and thinks the elephant a snake. The fourth thinks the elephant is a tree, the fifth, grabbing the elephant's ear, believes that the elephant is like a fan. The sixth and final man is *positive* that the elephant is like a rope. The whole story makes the men look foolish, but in many respects architects are expected to know the elephant. They are expected to start with a very limited and constrained perspective and make judgments about the whole enterprise.

In an architect's work, the whole enterprise is life itself. The hospitals we're born in, the houses where we raise our children, the schools we attend and the offices in which we've worked, are all conceived and driven by either the action or the inaction of an architect. The amount that an architect is expected to know about life and the minutiae of her clients' lives is extraordinary. A doctor is expected to know the human body, and a lawyer can be expected to know the law, but an architect is expected to have a working knowledge of anatomy, ecology, engineering, art, history, psychology, sociology, and bring that all to bear in her design process. She is expected to be a designer, a builder, a manager, an aesthete, a visionary, and a pragmatist at the same time. The amount an architect is expected to know borders on the absurd, and that is why design training focuses on methods to frame problems in responsible ways.

"Framing" is the act of deciding what is and what is not important in a design process; it is making a judgment about what's worth knowing. When you drive down the street, your eyes and your brain are rapidly consuming, processing, and dismissing large chunks of information. Your brain decides, often instinctually, what is and what is not important. A woman with a baby carriage crossing the crosswalk registers as an important piece of information, while the color of surrounding cars may not. On a relatively empty street, the color of cars may register as information, but on a crowded, high-speed street, your brain will likely filter that information out and instead focus on cars' relative proximity.

Our eyes and brains have evolved to work in such ways as a survival mechanism. Our well-developed brains mean that we have to be adept at filtering useless information from benign information from urgent, mortal information.

Our design process works in the same way, but perhaps less dramatically. Confronted with a design problem, we may find a great deal of information embedded within the site, the program, the client, and the surrounding city. The designer must choose what to respond to and what to ignore.

If a particular site was the location for a famous slave rebellion in the eighteenth century, and then in the nineteenth century was used as a chicken farm, the designer may design in a way that honors the slave revolt, or speaks to race consciousness in America, or to liberty, or to American ideals. There may be nothing in his design process that honors the millions of chickens that died on that farm. We regard this as okay—the designer made a choice and it feels like the right one. He has framed the design issues so as to exclude consideration of the chickens, but under the circumstances it is the right decision. To do otherwise would seem glib and offensive.

The difficulty with problem framing is that it accords the designer wide latitude in deciding what is and what is not a design consideration. It also allows an absence of knowledge to segue into an absence of concern. Such latitude can be a blessing, to be sure, but we have seen it yield disconcerting effects in recent architectural history. It has been used to exclude some drastic, urgent human problems from architectural discussion. It would seem that the tendency and authority to frame design problems is problematic—in uncertain hands, or in arrogant ones.

More problematic still, there seems to be no arresting influence in this series of exclusions. Architects still challenge each other, but in no systematic or universal way. It is possible to design to an idea, and, on the basis of a compelling visual and pure speculation, receive endorsement from the architectural community. Because architects can frame problems for themselves as well as for each other, a certain amount of skepticism can be removed from discussion. A state of not knowing does not necessarily mean that we're not designing.

Consider an idea that is increasingly prominent in the glossy architectural magazines: vertical farms. In concept, vertical farms deal with some fairly large and potent problems: mass urbanization, food supply, and the difficulty of feeding larger and larger urban populations. Moreover, vertical farms speak to the issues of sustainability that pervade our current urban/rural dichotomy. They are an attempt to reinvent how we distribute land and resources. Designers go to great lengths to explain the ecology, the hydrology, the circulation, and other merits. For all the profound ideas and all the beautiful renderings, there is hardly ever a discussion about urban real estate finance. Why? Because as designers, we do not want to be hamstrung by such gaudy considerations. To deal with them would only limit our creativity.

Complex financial analysis isn't necessary; common sense is. Average annual rental rates for office space in Midtown Manhattan hover around $60 per square foot. A single stalk of corn requires approximately three square feet of space, and the corn plant takes approximately eight months from planting to harvesting. In order for a vertical farm to generate rents equivalent to normal office space, the owner of the farm would have to sell the corn at approximately $120 per *ear*. Obviously, even in Manhattan, no farmer could sell corn for $120 per ear. The idea is completely unfeasible.

Does that mean that architects should stop designing vertical farms or ignore all the other questions that vertical farms explore? No. It does suggest that the omission of economic and financial questions will continue to keep vertical farms in the realm of urban fantasy, rather than of serious solutions to urban problems. By framing the problem to exclude inconvenient financial questions, we remove ourselves from the discussion. Someday, someone may indeed design a vertical farm that makes sense both ecologically and economically, but that design will arise out of a serious examination of both issues, not by favoring one and ignoring the other.

There is no way to know *everything*. We cannot contemplate being an expert designer, an expert farmer, and a financial expert at the same time. But we've already demonstrated that we don't have to. The only thing that is required is a resolve to design in a way that does not consciously exclude the inconvenient or the unpleasant. It is possible to design in such a way that we need not know the true nature of the elephant—our design provides for all six possibilities.

17 | You're an Architect, Aren't You?

I've heard this question many times, in a variety of arrangements. The most memorable occurrence found me in the Lower Ninth Ward of New Orleans while I was helping in an effort to establish a community design studio in the wake of Hurricane Katrina. The office in which I worked was a church that had loaned itself out for the reconstruction effort. With few parishioners resettled, the building found better use as a command post for first responders. The church had been converted into a community center that was part meeting place, part donation warehouse, part office building, war room, and design studio—all within four walls. Divisions between the center's various functions were accomplished with artfully placed furniture and file cabinets, when they were made at all. The church had had central air conditioning, but thieves had stolen the coils after the storm; the entire space was serviced by a couple of window units, to which I owe my life. With a floor of bare concrete and some donated furniture, a few hearty Lower Ninth residents moved mountains.

The facility, however, had sustained some damage, and being vaguely handy, I took it upon myself to occasionally tinker around here and there when things needed doing. This involved nothing from my architectural training, but a bit of elbow grease held over from my youth: some door hardware installed here, a lawnmower repaired there, and wherever else I could pitch in. As I was trying to pitch in, I found I was unwittingly diluting the "architect" brand.

The center was just getting on its feet, and one of the systems needing to be put in place was the phone system. I was asked to install it. When I acted puzzled, one of my coworkers—a native of the Lower Ninth—quipped, "Well, you're an architect, aren't you?" I didn't know how to explain that that wasn't exactly what architects did, and I didn't want to appear unhelpful, so I sat down to figure it out.

It wasn't anything particularly complicated. It was four phones and two lines. The system needed only to allow that all four phones could be in use at the same time, but truthfully the manufacturer had made most of the necessary provisions and supplied decent instructions to boot.

With a mixture of pride, astonishment, and chagrin, I did actually figure it out, probably cementing forever a misconception about architects, albeit to a limited audience. It left a large question in my mind about how architects are actually defined. Who is to say that architects don't install phone systems? Who owns that name? We have, in our own minds, a list of architects whom we consider "Architects." Our estimation of what it means to be an architect is probably largely shaped by whatever this mental canon of architects is doing. It is at once liberating and frustrating, as it gives us the freedom to define the name for ourselves, but also the responsibility. A responsibility which, if ignored, results in a name without meaning.

18 | The Named Architect

We must reclaim our name as an act of empowerment. To reclaim our name, we must focus on that which only we can do. Medical doctors are called medical doctors because the work they do is their exclusive province. No one else can lay claim to it, so the name is exclusively theirs.

Legally, an "architect" is someone who is registered and licensed by the state to practice architecture. This gives a right to carry the name, not a monopoly over the activity of design. To be a registered architect, one needs to complete a certain amount of educational training, a certain amount of professional training under another licensed architect, and the Architectural Registration Examination. This process can take as little as eight years.

However, the term is liberally applied to individuals who don't fit these criteria. Maybe rightfully so, depending on whom you ask. Nonlicensed architects can indeed design buildings, so long as they have a licensed architect stamp their drawings for them. An unlicensed architect may have many more years of experience and be much more talented than the person sitting next to her. However, if her cubemate is carrying a stamp, then only the cubemate can legally carry the title.

Architecture licensing in the United States is a state function. It is therefore legally possible to be an architect in one state but not in another. To complicate matters further, many projects now carry two architects: the *design* architect and the architect of *record*. Broadly speaking, the design architect is responsible for coming up with the schematic idea: the arrangement of space, the materiality, the massing, the texture, etc. The architect of record is responsible for producing the bulk of the construction documents and absorbs all the legal formalities of architecture, such as providing licenses, on-site work, insurances, etc. In essence, the architect's traditional body of design responsibilities is split between two different firms, allowing those firms to organize in different ways. A local firm with local knowledge can team with a firm of international regard, satisfying different priorities. From a professional standpoint, as long as the architect of record is licensed, insured, etc., it doesn't matter who the design architect is. The design architect need not necessarily be an architect in any conventional sense of that term. By the same token, the architect of record frees himself or herself from responsibility for the original idea.

Among the general public, misconceptions about architecture may get started in the media or the ether. Architects themselves, however, carry vague definitions of the term. Phenomena like the division between design architects and architects of record only serve to perpetuate the problem of defining architecture. Bernard Tschumi calls this split the "Third Dissociation," and opines that the split is disconcerting because it is part of "an historical evolution where the architect becomes more and more distanced from the forces that govern the production of buildings today."[1]

Another significant fissure is that between built architecture and "paper" architecture. The evolution of instant media did not create this rift, but it has perhaps irreversibly widened it. Instant, global media create the opportunity to extend an architect's visual reach beyond said architect's built work. An image can be manufactured, globally disseminated, studied, and revised in the time it takes to lay a single course of brick. This plain reality has given rise to a new profession: the paper architect. The term is often used derisively, but I use it merely to describe an aspect of our profession that allows one to become critically (and sometimes commercially) successful without being involved in the professional service of architecture or in the world of physical building. Prior to the modernist movement, a "successful" firm usually meant a firm that was successful along several dimensions: the most commercially successful firm was often the most critically well regarded. It might also have been the biggest. Large, powerful firms like McKim, Mead & White operated not only at elite commercial levels, but at elite critical ones as well.

The contemporary profession, however, operates quite differently. Large architectural firms like Skidmore, Owings & Merrill or Helmuth, Obata & Kassabaum do not enjoy the media celebrity status of a Frank Gehry or Rem Koolhaas. It is no longer necessary to be big or profitable in order to be considered successful. It is not even necessary to build.

The mediations between built success and paper success may seem ordinary to an architect. Analyzing the relationship is complicated by the fact that the terms themselves are subjective, but we can make a few simple observations. Quite simply, achieving built success is *harder,* or at least *rarer.* Producing either a groundbreaking design or a groundbreaking building requires years of iterations, blood, sweat, tears, layered upon a singularly brilliant idea. However, the former merely requires a sympathetic publisher or jury to establish its success; the latter also requires a sympathetic jury, but further requires millions of dollars, a sympathetic zoning board, a receptive public, good weather, etc.

If architecture is a steep pyramid of a profession, paper architecture and built architect can be seen as different pyramids—one steeper than the other. Paper architecture is a steep pyramid, but built architecture is a *really* steep pyramid. We know, of course, that these are not two completely separate things. They are not successive (you don't necessarily have to do one before you do the other) nor are they mutually exclusive (you can do both). However, we also empirically know that the two can be separated. An architect like Rem Koolhaas is known for both—his published works are as influential and celebrated as his buildings. An architect like Frank Gehry, however, is primarily known for his buildings, and publishes comparatively little. One like Lebbeus Woods is almost exclusively known for his printed material and visual conceptions of buildings.

This is not yet anything profound. But what *is* interesting to observe is the differential effects of paper success and built success. Both follow the mechanics of what Sherwin Rosen calls "superstar economics." In all professions, presumably, the higher in the field you rise, the more successful you are and the more money you make. But in superstar professions, these increases accelerate as you get nearer to the top. This distinguishes them from nonsuperstar professions, like optometry or accounting. If you are in the top one percent of all professional actors, you probably make millions of dollars; however, if you're merely in the top 10 percent, you probably only really make enough to support yourself. If you are in the bottom 50 percent, you probably are waiting tables to make ends meet.

Depending on the nature of the profession, success can scale quickly or slowly. But we have already acknowledged that paper architecture and built architecture scale differently. They are, in terms of superstar economics, *different* professions. If an architect is moderately successful in both professions—that is, as both a paper architect and a built architect—where should she focus her energy? She can pursue more paper architecture, because it's easier to be successful there, or she can pursue built architecture, which is harder but economically more rewarding. Hopefully, she will be pursuing both.

Now let us consider an architect who is a little more lopsided, one who is very well published and has produced a great body of unbuilt works. He does not have any built works, however. In the profession of built architecture, he is, in purely economic terms, unsuccessful. According to Rosen's logic, he would have to move very far up the scale in the profession of built architecture in order to realize any kind of success. It is the equivalent of a community golf course caddy contemplating a run at the U.S. Open. If he sticks to paper architecture, however, he can continue to be successful. For any given unit of work, his opportunities for success are much more palatable in the profession of paper architecture. Certainly he will continue to hammer away at the most prestigious design competitions, because, as we discussed, it's a means of vaulting himself into the world of built architecture. Fundamentally, though, the greater the paper success that he enjoys relative to his built success, the greater the incentive to stick with paper.

In an opposite example, another architect is highly successful in the profession of built architecture. She won some of her early work through competitions, but is established enough that she is frequently short-listed when a new project is proposed. How much time should she devote to making "paper" architecture? Broadly speaking, very little. A building speaks volumes, and, assuming it's well publicized, can do much more for her career than can a monograph full of unbuilt studio projects. She might occasionally enter open, international competitions, for the same reason sensible people may still occasionally buy a scratch lotto ticket, but practically speaking it makes more sense for her to build up her portfolio of built work and focus on the projects for which she has been short-listed. This may explain why many celebrity architects tend to publish less once they achieve built success. While they may have spent years or even decades in the paper world, once they have a practice focused on built work, Rosen's superstar theory predicts that they will continue to focus on built works.

We have created two professions that can seemingly exist independently. As long as they do, we can be confident of Rosen's model: the better you are at one relative to the other, the more sense it makes for you to stay in that profession. The wider the gap, the wider the gap wants to be. Therefore it is not enough to say that this architect will go his way and that other architect can go her own way, because every inch of space we put between the two begets a foot. We are creating two irreconcilable professions. We *cannot* choose one or the other.

By thinking of these two different kinds of perceived success as entirely different professions, we can observe that the gap between them is self-reinforcing. Despite the fact that some architects achieve both, by creating two different paths to the title of "successful" architect, we actually undermine a successful architecture. One detached from the other is more easily discarded than the two united.

These rifts and detachments, and the vagueness they are built on, begin in the academy. Architecture is unlike other professional disciplines in that you don't need to be a professional (in the legal sense) to teach in an accredited program. It is difficult to imagine someone teaching law on the single credential that they excelled at law school, but this nonetheless can occur at architecture school. Indeed, it is possible to move directly from a graduate education into a teaching position without any professional experience at all. In that sense, it is more like the academic disciplines, where one can move directly from undergraduate college to one's doctoral program to one's teaching career.

Many are surprised to find that several of the titans of twentieth-century architecture were never formally trained as architects: Le Corbusier and Behrens both went to art school, Frank Lloyd Wright only went to college for two semesters (part time), and Tadao Ando was formerly a truck driver.

The name can also be applied to individuals not associated with the built environment: individuals who write, or theorize, or make what would conventionally be understood as art. The term also possesses *qualitative* aspects. It can be used in a derisive or complimentary fashion, as in "Now, *that* is an architect" or "That guy's not really an architect, he only designs strip malls."

How can we summarize what we know about the name "architect"? An architect is someone with some minimum standard of training, unless he doesn't have it. An architect is someone who is recognized by the state as having some competency, unless she decides not to go that route, or she happens to be in another state. Or "architect" could mean someone who has designed something that has been built, unless he prefers the paper world. Finally, an architect is someone who designs well, as long as we understand that "well" is a relative and subjective term.

This seemingly includes anyone who has ever gone to architecture school, worked in an architecture office, designed something, talked or written about architecture. The professional difficulty with such a construction, as many architects understand, is that the term itself no longer means anything specific. "Architect" is the "aloha" of the modern professional landscape. There is no way to understand what the user is saying, unless the word is taken in context.

It is small wonder that misuse of the term is rarely sanctioned. Everyone agrees that there are certain minimum skills and training that a doctor should possess. If you don't possess those skills and training and represent yourself as a doctor, it is a criminal act. Depending on the circumstances of the case, you might very well find yourself going to prison. We cannot send people to prison for impersonating architects, however, if we ourselves can't agree on what the term means. With no definition to violate, it doesn't seem like a serious crime. Recently, a British newspaper reported,

> Acorn Building Design Associates of Mansfield have been ordered to pay a record £7,340 for breaching the Architects Act by using the title "architect" when not on the ARB [Architects Registration Board] register.
>
> Mansfield magistrates court heard that, despite warnings, the firm used the title in various advertisements and on its website. It was fined £5500 and ordered to pay £1840 costs.
>
> An ARB spokeswoman said: "At nearly £7,000 this was the heaviest penalty ever given to an individual or firm pretending to be architects. It reinforces the message that ARB will be

robust in protecting the title 'architect,' and the courts will punish those who deliberately mislead the public."[2]

The distinctions are now not only obvious but quantifiable. Impersonating a doctor: jail. Impersonating an architect: £7,000. It is notable that this was the *heaviest* fine ever assessed.

However, this is not the fault of the ARB or any other specific body. It arises out of the fact that you can't punish what you can't define. If we somehow jailed everyone who called themselves an architect but didn't meet that legal definition, some of our best theorists would be sharing cells with our most promising young professionals. The author would be penning this book from San Quentin. Luckily, our collective confusion over the term protects us all from possible incarceration.

The last time that we architects seemed to have a mild consensus about what the name "architect" meant and the activities it entailed was during the modernist period. For most of the first part of the twentieth century, there was relative agreement on the agendas, the methods, and the aesthetics of architecture. At the very least, lines were straight and angles were always right. With the decline of modernism, disagreement opened up about what architecture was and what architects should be doing. In Venturi's "complexity and contradiction" there was once again debate over what the name "architect" would stand for.

For many architects, the end of the modernist movement occurred on March 16, 1972. It was on this day that demolition began on the Pruitt-Igoe public housing project in St. Louis, Missouri. Pruitt-Igoe was completed in 1955, and had been receiving accolades for years prior. Designed by Minoru Yamasaki (who would go on to design the World Trade Center twin towers), the complex was seen as a new and innovative way to address the "problem" of the urban poor. Rather than being crammed into dark, twisted ghettos, the urban poor would be elevated in towers surrounded by parks, trees, and hope.

Within ten years, the complex was overrun with crime and physical decay. By 1968, residents were being asked to leave.

The Pruitt-Igoe's story, however, is not so simple as its timeline. Yamasaki's original design called for a mixture of garden apartments and high-rise buildings, not the uniform towers of the final design. The Public Housing Authority "forced" Yamasaki to double the density of the project from 30 units per acre to 55 units per acre.[3] Community spaces were excluded, except to the extent necessary to collect rent. Throughout the design process, "amenities" such as landscaping, painting the concrete block walls, and insulation on the scalding steam pipes were removed by the Public Housing Authority for budgetary reasons. It may in fact have been the interference of *non*-architects that led to the project's catastrophic failures.

Regardless, its story is held out as the largest and most dramatic failure of modernist ideals in the twentieth century. It became a pretext to move past the social agendas of the modern movement. The failure of modernism, as embodied by the 1972 destruction of the Pruitt-Igoe, seemed to be a psychological turning point within the profession—the point at which architecture ceased regarding itself as a means to an end, and started regarding itself as an end in itself. Before Pruitt-Igoe, architecture had been externalized in its attention. Modernism was ostensibly concerned with social change and utopia; earlier architectures variously concerned the glorification of God, or the emperor, or the state, or a wider culture, or a famous battle. In the early twentieth century, modernity asked us to discard and to reinvent, but it did so with some urgent technological and sociological imperatives. In the late twentieth century, postmodernism and deconstructivism canonized this need to discard and reinvent, but divorced themselves from the wider imperatives that had given anchor to all previous architectural styles. Koolhaas asked us to "break up the blacktop of idealism with jackhammers of realism and to accept whatever grows in its place."[4] The next architecture, it would seem then, must be *new*, but we won't take any steps to direct what comes about—we will "accept whatever." Beyond the debatable moral dimensions to this development, I believe this could be the last step in the complete dissolution of our name.

There are many architects who write morally about architecture's ideological evolution. They bemoan the recent developments as a symptom of the morally bankrupt "Me Decade." They issue calls to action and appeal to our better natures regarding architecture's moral role in the world. To their rivals, the "moral force" is only a symbol of architectural hubris—an idea that has been unequivocally shown to have been a failure. It is not necessary to settle this argument. Beyond issues of morality, we now face issues of professional survivability to which the profession must respond. Architecture must evolve—our very name is at stake and we cannot be nonchalant or accepting about what this will mean.

Many architects are already responding. Even in the early stages of the Great Wake, a flurry of op ed pieces have announced and/or denounced the end of celebrity architecture. The pervasive and hegemonic philosophies of architecture have eroded, and it is a time for many to sound off on what we think architecture should do. The king has passed on. A new one must be named.

The next architecture may be formally and aesthetically different, but we have every reason to believe that the laws of its formation will be the same ones that governed the creation of modernism, postmodernism, deconstructivism, etc.

Because the eighties, nineties, and the millennium were culturally governed by commerce, celebrity, instant persuasion, and immediate gratification, so too was our architecture. As our culture turns away from that ethos, our architecture will change as well. Not because of any moral imperatives, but because architecture will always, in subtle ways, reflect *us*, even when that reflection is unflattering.

Our architecture has been focused inward on architecture, not because celebrity architecture was somehow morally bankrupt, but because our culture demanded it. By the same logic, we can determine that architecture will now turn outward toward other things. Not because it should, but because it must.

As a first step, we must take back our name. The first step in reclaiming our name is to develop more specific definitions of what we do. But that will not be enough. We need to understand more about what we do. We need to isolate the things we do that set us apart from other professions—the skills that can't be duplicated, imitated, or cleaved apart. An architect may be a project manager, but a project manager is not necessarily an architect. We will set ourselves apart from these other professions when we identify problems that only we can solve. If what an architect can do is just a series of component processes that can be cleaved off and duplicated by other professions, it should be no surprise when our name is appropriated. So, what is it that only we can do?

Like one million of my fellow Americans, I saw Hurricane Katrina as a call to arms. The comfort of studio allows one to detach from many things, but this was one event that was hard to turn away from. Not that I wasn't tempted.

As the true scope and tragedy of Katrina unfolded, I was beginning another school year. While I just wanted to throw some things in the car and drive down there to help out, I was confronted with the ugly reality that I was, in fact, in studio, and I didn't have a car. I had some inkling that that was not the time for architects, anyway, and that the skills I had to offer would not be useful for at least another couple of months. I bided my time. Through the fall semester and the spring, I kept up with the news and made my plans. At the close of spring semester, I found myself heading south. I had little in my pack besides my laptop, a tent, and some bug spray, but I felt more secure in my direction than I had in years. The next three months would be an education. My first foray into the Gulf deserves its own book, and I couldn't do justice to the devastation that nature had wrought, or the heroism that was then rising where anonymity once stood.

My home for those three months was a small one-person tent. My residence there would change many of my understandings about home, shelter, and architecture, and I would never take air conditioning for granted again. Biloxi, in the summer time, is hot. Hot like I haven't the words to describe. Additionally, the storm had taken down a lot of the shade trees, and the air seemed to be all dust. The only things seemingly undisturbed were the crickets, who seemed capable of chirping, "Go away human, this is no longer a place for you" every time I had a moment of pause. That could have been the heat talking, though.

In our modern life, we often take it for granted that heat is escapable. I grew up in D.C., which can get pretty warm in the summertime, but every indoor space had air conditioning, and relief from the heat often meant just stepping into a home, a movie theater, or the closest Metro station. In post-Katrina Biloxi, there was no such relief—and it was an adjustment for the body. You sweat all day, then in the evening too. You sweat while you're eating, while you're showering, while you're sleeping. I ended up in the hospital at one point, unfamiliar as I was with the idea that you need to be drinking water all day, every day, just to get by. My tent reached 140 degrees during the daytime. Thankfully, I wasn't there during the day. At night, the tent cooled to somewhere between 90 and 100. I often slept with a Camelbak full of ice for a pillow.

Despite all these hardships, my heart was light. I felt I was getting in touch with architecture at its purest, most honest level. I was exploring architecture as shelter, as community, and as activism. I felt I finally understood what architecture was supposed to be about. I understood what a house was—it was safety, it was security, it was peace, health care, and the mark of a just society.

The New York Times *interpreted it differently. The* Magazine *was covering Steven Holl's latest: the Turbulence House for Mei-mei Berssenbrugge and Richard Tuttle. Author Michael Kimmelman cleverly juxtaposed a brief review each by Holl, Tuttle, and Berssenbrugge. Holl describes sleeping in the house: "The sun rises on the mesa from underneath you and the place glows with a gentle orange light that softly wakes you up." Tuttle offers a different view:*

The place is uninhabitable half the time. It's too hot in the summer, too cold in the winter. With lasers, they devised a footprint, a slab, on site, then when the panels arrived they didn't fit—they had to pull them together with straps, like a corset. Not very bright. Any damn fool knows you don't do these two things separately. I respect Steven. He's an artist. It's not his fault if the whole architecture profession is ego gone wild.

He adds:

It turns out that the greatest invention, the one that made civilization possible, is caulking.

Berssenbrugge is a bit more charitable, but still critical:

We wanted prefab, and instead we got a creative architect's iteration of prefab. It's not Green. It's not solar. It was twice over budget and construction was a nightmare and it's still not finished. But it is real architecture, and that's rare, with beauties only an artist can give you.[1]

Reading all this might leave a nonarchitect bewildered. How could someone be nonchalant about the fact that they just paid $600,000 for a house that is "uninhabitable" half the time? Such a result is probably a bit more understandable to an architect, but personally, the context was what stuck with me. As I was sweltering in the Biloxi heat, trying to define architecture for myself, the New York Times was defining it for the rest of the country. It splashed the Turbulence House across the cover of the Magazine, and despite the apparent oblique criticism by Kimmelman, a message was being sent. The path to fame, whatever its course, was apparently not affected by making houses that don't work, or houses that infuriate their owners. My lingering anxiety is that this dysfunctionalism "disinherits and preempts the birthright of successive generations of architects"[2] by saddling us with diminished expectations.

I was sitting in a broken plastic chair at the time I read the article, in the parking lot of another, different church that had been converted as a relief center and volunteer housing program. In the early evening, the heat of a Biloxi summer plays a number on you. It gets darker, and at some visceral level you expect it to cool down. But it doesn't. The heat hangs in the air for a few more hours like a bad date that won't end.

I was possessed by the thought that I had been failed by my antecedents—that they had set up for me a profession that existed only on the margins, that only flourished when the champagne was flowing. I felt that I had been disinherited not only of all architecture's noble missions, but of its day-to-day relevance as well. Watching the streams of volunteers returning from a day's work, I wondered if I had had it wrong.

I was left to meditate on this as I worked, in the blistering heat, with some of the most earnest and dedicated architects I've ever known. I worked with men and women who would likely never be on the cover of the New York Times. *Men and women who did not aspire to make a statement, or a "weird metal thing . . . that doesn't look like a house." Men and women who merely desired to use their skills to answer that basic human call of service. At night, falling asleep on a Camelbak full of ice, I would wonder whether service had any place in architecture— and whether architecture had any future without service.*

Architecture has no future without service. For that matter, it has no present without service, either. In the United States, at least, only an architect can design buildings, so long as those buildings are of a certain statutorily determined size and complexity. For many types and sizes of buildings, one cannot procure a building permit unless the drawings have been stamped by an architect. The architect, therefore, has a government-assured monopoly over some work associated with some projects. A great deal of our built environment passes through the hands of an architect. This same built environment gives rise to a number of ecological, economic, and social problems. Therefore, architects have a necessary, *statutorily regulated relationship* to some of our country's most severe problems. Depending on which architect you're talking to, or what project you're talking about, that relationship can be tenuous or ignored, but it is certainly always there. Those who have embraced this relationship often take the title of "citizen architect." This choice of term, however, ignores the inherent relationship of architecture to the social, economic, and ecological problems of this country. There are therefore only two kinds of architects: citizen architects, and *bad* citizen architects.

This claim is not as bold as it first appears. Consider the way we use the word "citizen" in the normal sense: for an individual who is part of some nationality or group. There are only a few possible exceptions to citizenship in this sense: one could be an illegal alien, or a prisoner of war, or a resident alien, or a tourist. None of these seem like an appropriate mantle for architecture or architects. And yet there are still architects who claim that citizen architecture and humanitarian causes lie outside of our responsibilities. What do these architects think they are, if not citizens? And if not *good* citizens, then *bad* citizens? *Inert* citizens? The whole claim is foolish.

Samuel "Sambo" Mockbee popularized the term "citizen architect" while a professor of architecture at Auburn University. There he founded the acclaimed Rural Studio at a time when most of the profession was looking inward. While mainstream architecture was trying to define itself amid a torrent of new technologies, formal possibilities, and cultural change, Sambo turned his students' attention to housing problems of the poor in rural Alabama. Altruistic endeavors in architecture had fallen out of favor, but the problems of the rural poor endured.

> The image of the architect shifted from social crusader and aesthetic puritan to trendsetter and media star. This change in professional definition had ramifications throughout architectural institutions. In the 1980s most schools stopped offering regular housing studios; gentleman's clubs, resort hotels, art museums, and vacation homes became the standard programs. Design awards and professional magazine coverage have embodied similar priorities. Advocacy architecture and pro bono work are almost dead.[1]

Citizen architecture describes an ethos; as there is no singular authority that can define for us what it means to be ethical, citizen architecture is similarly without an objective corner-stone. As we use the term here, the primary distinction between the citizen architect movement and the predominant architectural theory of the time is that the former advocated using architecture to solve problems beyond those relevant to architects themselves, their paying clients, or those who track Herman's "high" architecture. Citizen architecture is also distinct from the altruistic architecture attempted in the earlier part of the twentieth century. Sambo's efforts were not aimed at monumental, top-down solutions to society's problems; he merely asked his students to form a relationship with the communities that they were serving and ultimately became a part of.

It would be more accurate to describe this relationship as being "rediscovered" rather than "formed." After all, we are all inherently a part of our communities. Similarly, we are all part of our countries and of this planet. We are made so by being born. The only choice is whether or not to honor that identity.

Like many young architects, I came into architecture having been seduced by high modernist ideals and hagiography. In my early education, I counted many modernists among my heroes. As my thinking evolved, more and more of my heroes seemed to emerge from the relatively anonymous field of citizen architecture. In fact, as much as I admire Sambo et al., I was always a little disappointed in their choices of phrasing. Much of their writing casts humanitarian design, rural design, citizen architecting, etc. as subsets of an architectural dialog; they describe these problems as something we should be turning our attention to. I would rather they were described as the *only* issue in architecture.

By this I don't mean that every architect should spend every minute engaged in do-gooderism (although that's a wonderful world to imagine). But rather that every architect should, at every minute, be aware of the sociological implications of his or her choices. I believe it's possible for an architect to design a $300 million museum and still be a citizen architect, so long as he or she is conscious of the wider implications of his or her efforts. When an architect is given a $300 million budget for a museum and designs one that ultimately costs $320 million, does the architect ask where that extra $20 million comes from? Does it come out of the museum's budget for education programs? Does it come from the budget for collections? Suppose the museum is being funded by a foundation that also conducts other philanthropy. Does the $20 million mean fewer college scholarships?

Citizen architecting has become associated with a certain scale of project—and certainly not with $50 million museums. It may even be fair to say that Mockbee's message gets lost in the visual legacy of his work and the "move out to the woods and design with recycled car windshields" mythology. This, however, runs contrary to Mockbee's own words:

> In creating architecture, and ultimately community, it should make no difference which economic or social type is served, as long as the status quo of the actual world is transformed by an imagination that creates a proper harmony for both the affluent and the disadvantaged.[2]

Citizen architecting isn't necessarily tied to a certain type of client, project, or budget, so much as it is an awareness about the implications of what you're doing. Citizen architecture is often read as a reaction against the increasing nihilism and cynicism of the postmodern and deconstructivist movements. Postmodernism squirmed at the possibility that architecture might not be bound up in social responsibility. Deconstructivism reveled in it and used this freedom to explore new formal directions. The Nietzschean philosophical constructs that underpin deconstructivism reinforced the idea that architecture was an individual exploration done for its own sake.

This thinking renders architecture a cultural chamber of echoes—a series of tautological exercises whose only aim seems to be advancing itself critically. A discussion, as it were, about architecture and culture, conducted between architects but in buildings rather than words. In that sense, contemporary architecture is *aware* of very little. Not out of ignorance or some ineptitude, but because it chooses to be. It consciously chooses to marginalize the issues that had previously defined the profession.

You will find few people who will openly argue against the moral underpinnings of citizen architecture. It would just be tacky. However, in order to make the case *for* citizen architecture, we must also ask whether citizen architecture has a link to empowerment—does it make us stronger as a profession? Is there an immediate professional need to nurture and defend citizen architecture, as Dr. Miller saw the need to defend evolution in biological education?

Selling pet rocks aside, we generally derive value by creating some good or service that people find of use. Something that registers as important or necessary in their world. We do not get credit for solving our own problems. If I were to commission a custom-made suit, it would fit perfectly to my body, be of supreme comfort, and I would be willing to pay a lot for it. However, I would not pay the tailor a lot of money to craft a suit around *his* measurements, because such a suit is useless to *me*. In the same way, we must be mindful as architects that the problems we're solving are considered problems by at least *some* people outside the architectural community; solving problems that matter to nonarchitects is what gives our profession power.

The question of our responsibilities raged in twentieth-century architectural debate: Just how much is the architect expected to do for the benefit of mankind? Much of the early twentieth century, one could argue, was dominated by a techno-inspired altruism. Architecture was going to save the world, erase every slum, and draw utopia out of concrete and glass! A utopian confidence that came crashing down with Pruitt-Igoe.

Pruitt-Igoe was not a singular point in time, nor was it a black and white failure of any architectural theory, but it is helpful to understand that project's demolition as the end of the architecture's utopian social ambitions. Opponents of citizen architecture make the case that we tried and failed; that architects should stick to what they know best. They make the case that architecture must exclude global and altruistic missions if it is to flourish.

> The ideas of social progress and of man's ability to consciously construct his or her social world seem discredited today. Grand designs (as well as "grand narratives") are seen as nothing but grand pretensions, hubris with fatal consequences: "the fatal conceit."[3]

Whether or not architecture is better off since Pruitt-Igoe's 1972 destruction is certainly a matter of taste. The more urgent question is whether or not we will flourish in the *future*, given our current philosophical alignments.

If the profession of architecture collectively concludes that low-income or slum housing is not appropriate working material, can the profession survive as these issues loom larger and larger on the horizon?

To answer that question, consider a healthy, vibrant city: there should be many opportunities for an architect. Civic projects, infrastructure, housing, schools, offices, etc. all represent a canvas for architecture. And if there are a few slums lurking on the periphery of this city, the architect may be able to get away with saying, "Look, we tried dealing with that for fifty years, and we fumbled, it's clearly not something our profession should be dealing with—leave it to the planners or the politicians or the social workers." This reasoning may well be accepted, especially if the slums are out of sight from the new condos going up downtown.

But suppose now that those slums are growing. They are no longer on the periphery but are chewing their way to the center. Pockets of poor housing spring up here and there and the problem is getting harder and harder to ignore. Increasingly, the architect's disinclination to face the problem looks like plain indifference. However benevolent the initial intentions might have been (a suspect claim, to be sure), at some point the architect loses stock. He or she appears a mere aesthete who would prefer to work on issues of form, light, and tectonics as the rest of the world turns its attention to a massive, urgent problem. With barbarians at the gate, the architect is the one arranging flowers.

Politics and architecture have hardly intersected over the last generation, but they need to now. Leadership and design are essentially the same activity. They both require the creation, articulation, and defense of a vision—a proposal that there is some outcome that is superior to what currently exists. Like politicians, we must convince an audience that our vision is superior to the other guy's. Inherent to that is an awareness of one's environment. Politicians and architects have the same credibility requirement: they must be *in touch*.

We can declare with certainty that the problems of low-income housing, disaster housing, and slums are getting worse.

Simultaneously, our interest in them as a profession has waned. Globally, these problems are accelerating at a rate that almost defies quantification. The line between slum and city is blurring. And as these problems become more potent, an architect's refusal to address them puts our profession in peril. We will increasingly be seen as aloof and cynical.

It is a moot point to discuss whether architecture should have been looking at these issues all along. Moving away from them was perhaps a necessary reflex to changing societal and technological factors, or perhaps not. But to whatever extent we moved away from these issues, we must move back toward them now or risk being vilified.

In turning back to citizen architecture, we derive dual benefits: we stave off the vilification of our profession and we empower ourselves at the same time. We empower ourselves because, like a king, we demonstrate our talents. We show the world that we can take care of them, that we can assist in solving their problems, and that the tribute they pay us is returned to them in many benefits. We empower ourselves because we make ourselves necessary.

Like Dr. Miller's defense of evolution, we must pursue citizen architecture not just out of our moral natures, but out of our own professional self-interest.

I don't have much of an eco-footprint. It's not because I'm an eco-saint. I like to think of myself as incidentally green. I don't drive a car, because I can't afford the insurance or the maintenance. I don't pay much for utilities, because I'm not home that much. I also don't have many appliances, other than my laptop and my George Foreman grill. I sold most of them on Craigslist at one point or another to pay some bill or get some extra cash. I don't own a TV, or a watch, or a stereo. I tend to walk everywhere or take public transportation, because I usually find that I have a lot more time than money. I reuse old coffee cans as flowerpots, because flowerpots break and old coffee cans have an agrestic quality that appeals to me. What I've found is that when you don't have any money, you don't do very much. When you don't do very much, you tend not to have much of a footprint—ecological or otherwise. Being unemployed has made me green.

I can't escape the idea that to be more green, we just have to do less. As Americans, we have built a culture on using more than we need. Living in larger houses than we need, eating more than we should, driving more than we should, building more than we should, etc. It is this consumption that is at the root of our ecological problems.

Therefore, we may make the best impact through inactivity.

Doing less, as a phenomenon, ran particularly strong in the post-Katrina South. It was the "less" of the landscapes that grabbed my attention. Everything there was as it was pre-storm, less what it was supposed to do. So you had an auto shop, but no cars were being sold. You had a home, but no one lived there. A golf course where no one played golf. And a gas station that didn't serve gas. And yet all of these places were not inactive—they were alive with activity of the incidental and accidental kind.

The golf course had returned to nature. Wild grasses and weeds competed for open land. The only mark of civilization was the beginning of a tree house, built by a volunteer during a brief break. The course had become all rough.

The empty houses were basically functioning mold laboratories. And yet, at the very least, they served to inspire volunteerism, so maybe that's what they were actually growing. And the gas station had a small market, and functioned as a local meeting place. Amid swirls of dust, people chatted about who saw who do what. Unremarkable, except when you consider that the pools, the beaches, the pubs, and the traditional venues for socializing were in short supply. At the gas station, there was plenty of shade and beer and conversation.

This is an important design question. Designers spend effort trying to torture our physical environment to perform some function, to serve some purpose. Post-Katrina, with that purpose stripped away, new functions developed incrementally, passively, naturally.

All of this has troubling implications for architecture, to be sure. In many ways, the greenest building is the one we don't build. Fundamentally, we don't want to sit on the sidelines as our built environment returns to nature. We want a hand in how the environment is shaped, and are disinclined to approach the issue passively. We must engage green architecture with the conviction that our efforts are superior to what would occur passively. But we must root those convictions in honesty and openness—not in supposition and conceit. We must do what is best for our environment, even when that sometimes means doing nothing at all.

Like citizen architecture, green architecture is an opportunity for the architecture profession to help the world with its problems. Or at least to stop creating new ones. It is much more than just a trend or a fringe aspect of architecture. And it extends beyond just a technical adaptation or an embrace of new materials.

Green architecture is a sea change in architectural theory. It changes the priorities of what we do. Instead of examining questions or problems that are philosophical, or intellectually provocative, we are now looking at problems that are urgent and global. Like citizen architecture, it is something only we can do.

The origins of the green movement, in its widest sense, can be traced to Rachel Carson's seminal 1962 text *Silent Spring*. Other events serve as milestones in tracing the evolution of green theory: the first Earth Day in 1970, the Kyoto protocol in 1997, etc. When, exactly, architects began to pay attention to such issues is of considerable debate. As much trouble as architects have in defining "design," they find defining "green design" even more difficult.

A full definition, therefore, will remain elusive, at least within the pages of this book. To understand how green architecture relates to architectural empowerment, however, we would be wise to at least define what green architecture is *not*.

The most widely accepted definition of sustainability was conceived at the United Nations Brundtland Commission in 1989 and reads: "[to meet] the needs of the present without compromising the ability of future generations to meet their own needs."

According to the UN, then, sustainability seems to be about meeting needs. We can believe that a "green" building is one that satisfies the needs of the present without imperiling the needs of the future. But *whose* needs? The needs of the client? The architect? The public at large? The spotted owl that lives in the forest where the flooring is harvested? Some architects would say "all of the above." But the plain truth is that in most scenarios, someone's needs come first. Depending on who your architect is and who your client is, someone may be getting the short end.

Perhaps it is easier to look to the specific language of the Brundtland Commission: ". . . without compromising the ability of future . . .". The Commission makes no claim to be *meeting* the needs of future generations; it does not stipulate that it is squirreling away clean air or clean water or anything specific. It does not even appear to be taking a position on whether or not those future generations will rise to meet their *own* needs. It merely declares that we shouldn't act in a way that precludes them from doing so.

To understand this in architectural terms, we might speculate that "sustainability" means designing in such a way that we do not imperil the future fortunes of three parties: future architects, the client, and the community at large.

Intuitively, this seems correct. We would never consciously design a building that would fall apart in three years. We know that regardless of what we might be doing in three years, or where the world may take us, it is probably to our advantage that that building is still standing. It is certainly to our client's advantage that the building stay up as long as possible. Similarly, we would not design a building that looks good on opening day and then fades aesthetically. Designers give careful thought to how materials age—they may select copper knowing that the patina which will rapidly take hold is the look they are going for. A designer may eschew untreated concrete because he or she knows that subsequent staining may spoil a meticulously crafted image. So, technologically, we would want to design in a way that does not imperil our future reputations.

Aesthetically, we face similar issues. A designer may engage a new and revolutionary material out of critical or intellectual curiosity; or perhaps because a newly invented material offers new possibilities. Whatever the case, it can work out very well for the architect. We can look back on that designer and say, "What a daredevil! Look how he explores!" Le Corbusier and his whitewash and Gehry with his chain link fencing were separated by a couple of generations, but both gained fame through adventurous choices. We recall them as the first to make such choices. Notably, these choices do not prevent future generations from making similarly adventurous choices. Formal choices, as well, are easily outdone. A decision to make a building in the shape of a seahorse does not directly bind future generations of architects in any way.

The client's future becomes bound much more easily. Future generations of *designers* seem fairly unencumbered by a particular design choice, but future generations of clients, or neighbors, or the general public will continue to be affected until the building is taken down. If a school is designed with poor natural lighting, the school district may be burdened with additional energy costs for the life of the building. *Every* generation that moves through that school will be similarly affected. Every taxpayer that lives in that district will be affected. A designer's choices have become *binding* in a very real way.

The similarities between green architecture and citizen architecture here start to emerge. They both require a heightened sense of awareness on the part of the designer. They both ask the designer to take responsibility for how the client and the community are affected, not just in the honeymoon period but in perpetuity. We must design in such a way that a building can be a source of continued value for the client and the community at large far into the future.

This is easier said than done, because the mechanics of the profession as it is currently organized work against such long-range thinking. Architects are rewarded for making something new—for departing from what has been established and proven workable. Any notable architect achieves his or her position in the canon specifically by diverting from an existing dialog. Moreover, that position is evaluated and secured at a single point in time; the reactions of subsequent generations are typically not controlling in the evaluation of an architectural work. We may regard a fifty-year-old building as something ugly and dated, but still celebrate the architect who designed it because at the time it was a bold gesture.

This raises an obvious question: if a designer designs a building that is formally or aesthetically trendy for his own generation, what happens in the next generation, when the trend fades? What is the owner left with? A dated building that is as awkward to own as a mood ring is to wear? If the building in question is a home, is the owner left with a resale option? Is the owner's equity destroyed because the architectural trend that inspired the building has passed and now no one can be convinced to buy it? This issue is perhaps more confusing now than ever before. For most of human history, historicist forces in architecture insured that the architect's primary duty was to reference the past, thus ensuring some measure of continuity between the generations. In an era when every generation's ambition is to part from the past, how do we make sure that we allow for future generations' needs—when the only certainty is that they will be actively trying to distinguish themselves from us?

Perhaps it is enough to say that, rather than trying to decipher the "then," we will just try to deemphasize the "now." Buildings should not be subject to fleeting trends or inspired by flash-in-the-pan ideologies; as put (ironically) by Daniel Libeskind: "When we talk about sustainability, it should be seen as something genuine, not trendy or technically gimmicky."[1]

We should not design our buildings to reflect the Me Decade, or *any* decade, because we want our buildings to be meaningful and useful in the *next* decade. We want future generations to have some use for them, rather than have them just stand as cultural markers of our own particular moment in time.

Green architecture, then, would seem to lend itself to conservatism: the safest way to achieve its goals is to stick with what has proven to be workable and generally tolerable. To design in such a staid way is problematic for two reasons:

• It runs counter to the mechanics of fame and success in our profession.

• It runs counter to the march of technology.

To the first point, we must find a way to make the mechanics of success of an individual gel with the mechanics of success of the profession. As I have said, we have, for too long, believed that the success of a few individuals necessarily translates into a strong and healthy profession. The fallout from the Great Wake suggests that this is not true. When the public at large understands that sustainability is a core value to all architecture, and that architects take seriously their role in this crisis, we all benefit. If the public suspects that architects are using the issue of sustainability as a gimmick, to advance their own portfolio and dabble in new technologies, the public will be understandably suspicious. We must consider architecture in such a way that doing the right thing is more lauded than doing the new thing. We will always be called upon to do things in new ways—shifting times and technology demand it—but we must give up the idea of newness for its own sake. Only then can a real discussion of sustainability be had.

To the second point, such a contradiction can be resolved by considering a simple piece of technology: my USB thumb drive. I got my first one a few years after college. It had 128 Mb of memory and cost almost $100. I can't remember all the USB drives I've had over the years, but I do know that they have steadily achieved more and more memory. They have also become less and less expensive, when considered in terms of dollars per byte of memory. My current one (which is now at least 18 months old) provides 2 Gb of memory and cost me around $30.

At what point do I decide to replace it? I consider two factors: the advance in technology and the drop in price. If I were to buy the most advanced, highest-memory thumb drive I could find, I would do so with the knowledge that it would only remain state-of-the-art for a brief time. The curve of technology is accelerating, and making a purchase represents an act of "getting off the train." Thumb drives will continue to have more and more memory, but the one that you have has the same memory capacity as it did the day that you bought it. Therefore, a "tech gap" between what is state-of-the-art and what you own is always widening.

The falling cost of a technology is also an incentive for me to replace my thumb drive. We have all experienced the heartache of buying some new piece of technology and watching, sometimes over a period of only months, as the price dropped and dropped. If I paid $30 for a 2 Gb drive a year ago, and now a 4 Gb drive is available for $15, it makes a compelling argument for replacement, even if the old one is still working fine.

Because the "tech gap" is always rising and the price is always falling, there is always a distinct calculable point at which these two lines intersect. At this point, it makes more sense for me to replace my thumb drive than it does to hold on to the last one. Eventually, technology always inherently demands its own replacement.

This has been an oversimplified example. Our purchasing (replacing) decisions are never strictly a matter of cost and technology, but also involve fashion, market externalities, consumer price index, etc. However, the example adequately illustrates how chasing state-of-the-art technologies can inspire us to replace our possessions at a rate that defeats any efforts at sustainability.

For this reason, a faith in green technology is easily misplaced. We might design a high-performance building that represents the peak of current technology, but we have to acknowledge that the technologies themselves rapidly lose their state-of-the-art status and correspondingly their value. The greater the divergence between our high-performance building and the state of the art, the higher the pressure to *replace* the building.

Such a phenomenon suggests that a faith in "green" might be more appropriately based on passive technologies. The sun will likely follow the same arc one hundred years from now as it does today. The winds will blow generally in the same direction. Utilizing technologies dependent on sun and wind ensures that the benefits of our design decisions endure over the long term, rather than being undermined by economic and technological phenomena.

Ruskin believed that "a building cannot be considered as in its prime until four or five centuries have passed over it."[2] In his time, such an approach might have worked. The times changed much more slowly. These days, such a long time scale may be wishful thinking, especially considering the aforementioned accelerating pace of technology. Indeed, such foresight may be impossible unless we are current or future historicists. But we can make certain decisions that allow for future generations to also make fruitful decisions. We can design with materials that, after the building has served its useful life, can be taken down and reused. We can design around ideas and events that are lasting, not short-term cultural phenomena. We can design buildings around "existentially grounded plastic and spatial experience" rather than "the psychological strategy of advertising, of instant persuasion, [where] buildings have turned into image products detached from existential sincerity."[3]

We can design buildings to *last*, rather than defaulting to a thirty-year useful life estimate. Above all we can culture an awareness of how our buildings will affect the future—architecturally and ecologically. We can elevate durability over technology.

If you were a kid growing up in the eighties in DC, there were many places you weren't allowed to go. One place you really weren't allowed to go was 14th Street. At night. That's because 14th Street, at night, was for hookers. As a kid, I barely understood what prostitution was, what might be wrong with it, and I certainly had no practical use for a prostitute. But I knew enough to stay away from 14th Street. Somewhere around the late eighties and early nineties, the street cleared up. The cleanup roughly coincided with my teenage awakening to the fact that girls were, in fact, present on Earth and also with my first flirtations with the market economy. I was beginning to do a little work and have a little cash flow. It was perhaps a fortuitous misalignment of events. It also aligned chronologically with a general "cleaning up" of the city, or perhaps a "gentrification," depending on your point of view. Whatever the case, the 14th Street prostitution corridor up and went, so to speak.

Many years later I met a local historian who confessed a theory. I'm not sure if it made more sense than the other theories I had heard, but it was full of intrigue and therefore was much more interesting to me than banal economic explanations. His theory involved the Cold War, spies, wiretapping, prostitution, corruption, and probably some other vices that I have forgotten. The theory was that the 14th Street prostitutes were protected by the CIA. The District, being a center of international politics, was constantly visited by diplomats, dignitaries, lecturers, heads of state, etc. These visitors were almost exclusively male and well-to-do. When they came to town, away from their countries, wives, and local medias, they would indulge in the local flavor, so to speak. While the Cold War was going on, this was great spy business. The CIA merely had to bug the bordellos or motels that the prostitutes were using, and essentially throw one big blanket over the entire international community.

If the prostitutes were in jail, however, the visiting johns would have nowhere to go. They might be tempted to stay in their embassies and get work done. So it was in the interest of the CIA to keep the prostitutes busy, working, and unfettered. According to my friend, the CIA leaned on the local police to ignore the prostitution problem, in the interest of national security.

Once the Cold War ended, the utility of the prostitutes was diminished. The CIA withdrew its protection, and the prostitution problem gradually was eliminated by local law enforcement. Now there are a Best Buy and a Target on 14th Street.

Prostitution is called the world's oldest profession. It exists in every city, in every culture, and in every age. In economic terms it is useful, as proved by its ubiquity. It is presumably always beneficial to the client, but in other circumstances, apparently, becomes useful in its externalities. In the case of 14th Street, protecting national security. Under certain circumstances, it becomes really useful, and we watch it proliferate accordingly. Architects can take a lesson.

24 The Sober Architect (or, A Doctor, a Lawyer, and an Architect Walk into a Bar)

An architect, a lawyer, and a doctor walk into a bar. The doctor sidles up to the bar and says, "I have no money, but I will trade you a free physical for a pint of ale." The bartender scratches his head for a moment and realizes that this is a really good deal, then serves up a pint. The lawyer also is out of money, but offers to sue someone on the bartender's behalf. The bartender chuckles and remarks that, as a bartender, he has few enemies. However, he has an elderly mother that needs a will prepared and he would trade such legal services for a pint. The lawyer thinks that sounds okay and agrees to the deal.

The architect hears all this and offers to design a house for the bartender, for the cheap price of a pint of ale. The bartender looks at the architect for a minute trying to decide whether or not the architect is serious. After realizing that the architect wasn't joking, the bartender sheepishly confesses that he doesn't need a house designed, he already has one. The architect, watching his friends enjoying libations, changes his offer: "I will redesign your bar for the price of a beer." The bartender again scratches his head and replies, "There's nothing wrong with the bar. The bar has been like this for thirty years, everyone loves it here. It's reassuring." The architect, getting increasingly frustrated, explains that he could design it better—that it could be safer and cleaner and more modern and more provocative. Instead of a bunch of dead wood and tarnished metal, it could be made of modern, green materials that evoke meaning and ask questions!

The bartender is starting to get more amused than confused, but explains to the architect that all those things that the architect is objecting to are *the things that actually draw in his customers.* They like the fact that the décor never changes—it provides a sense of stability and consistency. He explains that his customers come here year after year—they get married, they get divorced, they get fired, they get promoted—and they come to *his* bar to celebrate life's victories or to drown their sorrows. They come to be around friends and small comforts, not to be challenged by postmodern questions arising out of an architect's choice of materials.

Now convinced that the bartender is a rube, the architect tries to explain it a different way. The doctor offered you a physical, which might cost at most $200, and the lawyer offered to draft a will, which might cost at most $400, and each of them received a beer for their trouble. The architect crows that he is offering to design a house, or redesign the whole bar—a professional service that would run in the tens of thousands of dollars—and it is impossible to believe that those services are not worth one single goddamn beer.

The bartender apologizes, but again reminds the architect that those are not services that he needs. They are not worth thousands of dollars *to him.* And he cannot be convinced that they are worth something. The architect goes thirsty.

Collectively, we must understand what our profession is worth, who needs it, and why it is valuable. Not everyone will need our services; after all, "An architect is more likely to hire a prostitute than vice versa."[1] But many more people could be benefiting from our services, and our profession could grow stronger as a result.

The modernist conclusion that *everyone* needs our services, even when they don't want them, and the deconstructivist position that we aren't obligated to provide services to anyone or anything besides architecture, both seem equally flawed today. Amid the Great Wake, we must step out of our architects' shoes to talk about architecture. We must occasionally see architecture with a layperson's eyes, to understand its place and how it is valued. We do not diminish or dishonor ourselves in doing so; we only humanize ourselves. We must understand that design can't solve every problem, but not let that become a pretext to abandon our role as problem solvers.

De Botton's conclusion that "the noblest architecture can sometimes do less for us than a siesta or an aspirin"[2] rang in my ears throughout many late nights in studio. And during my service in New Orleans and the Mississippi Gulf Coast, as the sun would set on a long, sweaty day of frustrations, I'd be much more interested in seeing a siesta *and* an aspirin than I was in seeing any architecture materialize.

As a profession, we find it hard to own up to this. We keep our own counsel on how important architecture is, how majestic, and how fruitful. We rarely challenge the specter that architecture might not be worth much, because we never challenge anyone who's of that opinion. We hang out with other fans of architecture. And those who aren't fans—who don't see value in design—are dismissed with a wave of the hand. We have become a *narcissistic* profession, in the clinical sense. The arbiter of what is right and what is wrong is merely our own collective inclinations. We justify the rightness of our actions by the fact that *we* did them. We become great designers by virtue of making great designs, and when asked how we know they are great designs, the answer is simple: *because we are great designers.*

We are validated by the fact that our colleagues like our work, and sometimes our clients as well. I have tried to make the case that this is not enough. While there is and always will be potential for any one of us to be successful within this profession, it is less clear that the profession itself will be successful. There is considerable evidence that we have been significantly marginalized—and will be further marginalized still. It is doubtful that society will allow our self-indulgence to continue. Surely, in the face of global climate change, critical mass urbanization, and economic meltdown, the world will not be interested in the musings of a profession that is conceptually out of reach and morally silent. The world needs *kings*—and will no longer tolerate sorcerers.

As I struggled to pen the final pages of this manuscript, the ceiling above my desk began to leak—a decidedly nonregal turn of events. The final pages were written while I squatted in a tiny sublet in St. Louis, my third residence in six months. My partner and I had found a deal on a summer sublet and it seemed to be a convenient place to hole up and look for work. After we had moved in, we learned that the reason rents were so cheap on that particular street was because it was heavily populated by adult group homes for the mentally handicapped, a fact we discovered after noticing that our slightly agitated but relatively harmless neighbors seemed to have no other occupation than walking up and down the block repeatedly and waving. The rents were low because most people are uncomfortable living among such a density of the handicapped, I supposed, but personally I found it comforting. My neighbors were always waving and smiling and asking me how my day went. I never had much good news to report, but it never seemed to bring their spirits down or quell their inquisitive natures. I adopted them as my cheerleading section.

They were of little help with my leaky ceiling, though. Without particularly thinking about it, I immediately understood that the drainage tube from the window AC unit in the apartment above ours had been bumped or misdirected. It wasn't draining to the outside, as it was supposed to. It was draining into the wall cavity, and then to the floor cavity, through the plaster, and finally down onto my desk. I watched the stain on the ceiling widen like a bruise over the course of the day. Unfortunately, we couldn't call the landlord to have this problem fixed. We were there only semilegally—the previous tenant had moved out and let us move in without telling his landlord. It was never clear to us whether the previous tenant was actually allowed to sublet the place. To call the landlord would have been to open this particular can of worms, and we would have had to explain why his previous tenant had moved out, and why he now had two people, two cats, and a bird living there.

So I didn't call the landlord. And I didn't fix the leak. I took two of our remaining three pots and set them up on the desk to catch the dripping water and got back to writing. The steady drip kept me company as I drew out the thoughts that would come to be my personal statement on the economic crisis and its consequences for architecture.

In a way, the dripping ceiling was every bit as serendipitous as my encounter with Detour Road. Here was a problem—a simple one—one that I knew how to fix, and yet through a collusion of unfortunate circumstances I was powerless to do anything about it. I was no more in a position to fix the leak than I was to practice architecture.

My dad had taught me as a kid exactly how to fix this sort of thing when our roof leaked. My reaction was the same as it was every time he undertook a project: "Daaaad, can't we just call a repairman?" The answer was always no; he was from *that* generation. He had grown up a farm kid and, despite having ten

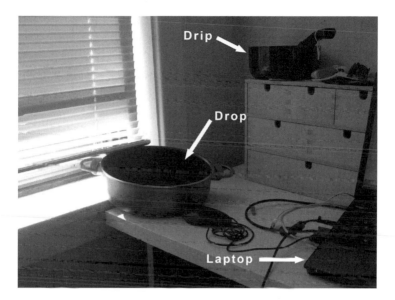

Figure 25.1
Improvising architecture.

years of higher education, instinctively reached for his toolbox, not the telephone, any time the house presented a problem. Getting dragged in to assist on these household projects was a regular childhood trauma, but one of the ones you look back on wistfully. They taught me to work with my hands—that sense of craft that every architect needs. They taught me a little building science. And, by way of the hardware store, I found a reverence for architecture.

The hardware store was a nineteenth-century row house, a design and construction typical for that era in that neighborhood. The entryway was laid in tiny, intricate tile—the kind fashioned by successive waves of poor but talented European craftsmen, who immigrated in droves throughout the nineteenth century and brought their craft traditions with them. The storefront was a glorious wave of copper, like the entrance to a temple or a mystic vault, and the door was so heavy my dad had to open it for me. The staircase had a thick, coiling banister that, in my young hands, always felt as thick and wild as an anaconda. My father would busy himself trying to find a widget or a sprocket or whatever that day's project required, and I was relatively free to wander about the store and indulge my childish fantasies. I was still at an age when I had enough imagination to be free and enough learning to internally articulate my fantasies. I could imagine myself a pirate, cavorting about a hidden fort. Or a knight, exploring theretofore unknown rooms in a massive castle. Many years later I would find myself in school paying tens of thousands of dollars trying to redevelop the creativity which at age ten seemed to come so naturally. Its rambling and unchallenged nature would run spiritedly, painting whole worlds over simple canvases. In this case, I had more than a simple canvas—I had a rich panorama, and my fantasies were appropriately detailed.

I didn't know anything about architecture in those days, but the detailing and the richness of the place were fertile ground for a young imagination. There was a gravitas about what went on there, the way that a dusty, tattered leather cover grants weight to the content of the pages within, even when they are something mundane.

Many years later, during thesis semester, I would find myself on a late-night run to Home Depot, seeking materials for some model that I was going to build for some purpose that at the time seemed like a big deal. Awash in the timelessness of studio culture, I didn't find the harsh fluorescents disturbing. My bloodshot eyes and coffee circles were more or less permanent during that phase of my life. Day could have been night and night could have been day; it was all the same to me. My location was never important, either, except for the fact that I wasn't in studio. Even more alarming was that my environment seemed to fit me so well a zombified, malnourished thirty-something shopping for copper wire at 9:30 at night did not raise any alarms. In fact, it was as if the Home Depot were developed specifically around my needs. Far from feeling comforted, I felt suddenly displaced. The fact that my lifestyle could be so distorted—that my schedule and my diet and my priorities could be so out of kilter—and yet the "architecture" around me still seemed to work set off a pop in my head like a broken tooth. I was a few decades and 1,500 miles from the hardware store of my youth, and it occurred to me: when I have kids and I take them to the hardware store, they will not experience architecture, as I had. They will experience Home Depot. I think that's ultimately why I wrote this book—because I don't want them to grow up in a world where they have to go to a museum to experience architecture.

I want them to find richness and imagination in their built environment. I want them to find beauty in the everyday: in simple detailing and honest efforts. I don't think that they'll find that at Home Depot. They'll find aisles that are twenty feet high—designed around commerce instead of human scale. They'll find sterile VCT floors and harsh fluorescent lighting that, especially at 9:30 PM, reveals more of your blemishes than it does of your imagination. And they'll find an assault of orange. The color of safety.

My kids will not have a say in the matter, because Home Depot has become everyone's hardware store. Over twenty years or so, it crept up from a rural or suburban experiment into the only hardware store left. In the same way, Best Buy replaced the local electronics store. Manufactured housing replaced craft, and while I was in grad school Walgreens replaced the local drugstore at a rate of one new store every eighteen hours. These shifts were economic. They occurred because we live in a value society—where the store that gives us the most for the least is going to prosper, and all the rest will fade into oblivion.

The last thirty years of Architecture (with a capital A) seem to have done little to challenge this. At best, architecture has positioned itself as a critical observer of this transformation, doing little to steer its course. There were of course dissenters, and I have tried to name a few in these pages. But it was thick monographs that made it to the coffee tables, not somber prognostications. The most vocal architectural discussion has centered on issues of form, process, tectonics, and materiality. The market, however, resoundingly and furiously answered these questions, at least with regard to hardware stores. While architecture was asking itself some pretty complicated questions, the market went on ahead with a fairly simple solution.

It will surely be argued that this is not so grave a development. That "real" architecture is not about hardware stores, and that other programs offer more fertile ground for experimentation and progress. In my mind I return to Dr. Miller and his Harvard student, and ask where this progression leads. We have nurtured a culture in which people don't care about architecture in their hardware stores, inspired instead by the prospect of saving $0.25 on a package of nails. Judging by the proliferation of McMansions and other embarrassments, most people don't value architecture in their homes either. Nor in their electronics stores. How long before they don't value architecture at all?

If it is our future to be consigned to the hall closet of apathy, then the Great Wake is the turning of the doorknob. Given how little our culture seemed to care about architecture when the credit was flowing, it is easy to imagine that in the new economy architecture will disappear completely. Tighter credit rules and greater expectations will prompt people to ask, with greater seriousness than ever before, "What value am I getting for my money?" Architects have always had a hard time answering that question, because at some level we will always be dealing with phenomena that cannot be quantified in dollars and cents. We deal in beauty and culture and meaning, and to try to quantify those things in dollars is not only gauche but impossible.

That will not, however, stop people from asking. They will ask, and when we have no answers they will build McMansions and Home Depots. In a way, they have been asking the same question all along—at least as far back as modernism. Back then we answered confidently: architecture was valuable because it was going to save the world—moreover, it was the only way to save the world! More recently, we have done our best to ignore such questions. In a credit-based economy, we could. Those who were our fans and patrons had good credit, and it wasn't their money they were using anyway. It was the bank's money, or the public's money. And when the bank ran out of money, we know now, it would just ask the public for more.

To outline the specifications of a new direction in architecture, we can begin by believing, with some certainty, that the questions (both financial and architectural) that have been ignored for thirty years will start to be asked again. It is these questions that gave rise to the ten architects described in this book. Each of the ten is a response to a particular question, whether about architecture's value, its risk, or its purpose. They are only responses, though, not answers. The answers will come when we find some means of explaining and defending our value that doesn't rely on the public's belief that we are experts and that our judgment is beyond reproach. The titans of Wall Street made the same mistake. For years we heard, "We are the experts, we know what we're doing, your opinion doesn't matter, leave us alone." It is safe to say that the world will no longer tolerate this attitude in its financial system, or in its government. Why would it tolerate it from its architects?

I look forward to a world where every building is Designed. Every building has the mark of an architect and every person can wake up to a beautiful home, a well-planned city, a humane school or workplace. In a sense, I am still hanging on to the modernist dream. Which isn't to say that I am unaware of the mistakes the modernists made, or have any particular fondness for their aesthetic. But to reject modernism's altruistic ambitions along with its formal stylings and (admittedly autocratic) politics is to resign from society. It is to position oneself outside. As observer, or critic, or hermit, or recorder, but never as citizen, never as a leader.

I look forward to a world where people care about architecture again. Not just critics and students, but everybody. Not just in their museums and city halls, but everywhere. I believe this world is possible. I believe that our present economic crisis is fertile ground in which to plant some seeds. But for them to care about us, we have to start caring about them. We have to believe that ideas like finance, risk, citizenship, and sustainability fall within the purview of the architect. To ignore such issues is to say to the world, "We do not care about what is important to you." We can expect the world to answer back, "Very well, we don't care about architecture." Perhaps it already has. The thought scares me from time to time, but I take comfort in the fact that throughout the twentieth century, whenever the world has descended into true economic calamity, a new architecture has arisen. I feel blessed that my generation will have an opportunity to rise to these challenges and be a part of whatever comes next. My generation will have the opportunity to be true "shapers" because they will reshape not only the formal aspects of architecture, but how we practice and, more importantly, why we practice.

A friend asked me recently whether the economic crisis had changed me, and I confessed that it had. It has made me more optimistic. I don't have any more job prospects or money than I had when I graduated, and I don't expect the crisis to resolve anytime soon. But my personal search has been sewn up nicely. I found my architecture, and I'm making my own road these days.

Notes

Chapter 2

1. Peter Eisenman, "The End of the Classical: The End of the Beginning, the End of the End," in Kate Nesbit, ed., *Theorizing a New Agenda for Architecture: An Anthology of Architectural Theory* (New York: Princeton Architectural Press, 1996), p. 223.

2. Annie Choi, "Dear Architects," *Pidgin* 2, no. 2 (2007), pp. 266–269.

3. Ray Porter, *The Greatest Benefit to Mankind* (New York: W. W. Norton, 1997), p. 349.

4. Ibid., p. 351.

Chapter 3

1. Robert Fielden, "Changing Roles for Architects: Regulation vs. Art," in William Saunders, ed., *Reflections on Architectural Practice In the Nineties* (New York: Princeton Architectural Press, 1996), p. 121.

2. Andrew Shanken, *194X* (Minneapolis: University of Minnesota Press, 2009), p. 7.

3. Eugène-Emmanuel Viollet-le-Duc, *Discourses on Architecture* (Boston: James R. Osgood, 1875), p. 474.

4. Lords Esher and Llewelyn-Davies, "The Architect in 1988," *RIBA Journal* 75 (October 1968), p. 450.

5. Andrew Saint, *The Image of the Architect* (New Haven: Yale University Press, 1983), p. 68.

6. Pierre Pellegrino, "Educating Architects," in Martin Pearce and Maggie Toy, eds., *Architecture: A Social Philosophy and a Spatial Skill* (London: Academy Editions, 1995), p. 59.

7. Jack L. Nasar, "A Post-Jury Evaluation: The Ohio State University Design Competition for a Center for the Visual Arts," *Environment and Behavior* 21, no. 4 (1989), pp. 464–484.

8. Herbert J. Gans, "Toward a Human Architecture," in Judith Blau, Mark E. La Gory, and John S. Pipkin, *Professionals and Urban Form* (Albany: State University of New York Press, 1983), p. 308.

9. Steven D. Levitt and Stephen J. Dubner, *Freakonomics* (New York: Harper Collins, 2005), p. 90.

Chapter 4

1. Witold Rybczynski, *The Most Beautiful House in the World* (New York: Viking Penguin, 1989), p. 82.

2. Curriculum requirements paraphrased from the University of Buffalo Master's in Urban Planning Program (www.ap.buffalo.edu/planning/degrees/mup.asp).

3. An example from the University of Michigan, available at http://taubmancollege.umich.edu/ud/courses.html.

Chapter 6

1. Paul Krugman, *Peddling Prosperity: Economic Sense and Nonsense in the Age of Diminished Expectations* (New York: W. W. Norton, 1994), p. 96.

2. Ibid., p. 79.

3. Ibid., p. 4.

4. Michael Boyle Bernard, "Architectural Practice in America 1865–1965: Ideal and Reality," in Spiro Kostof, ed., *The Architect* (New York: Oxford University Press, 1992), p. 341.

5. Jason Timberlake and Stephen Kieran, *Refabricating Architecture: How Manufacturing Methodologies Are Poised to Transform Building Construction* (New York: McGraw Hill, 2004), p. 53.

Chapter 10

1. $P(x) = n![n!/[x!(n - x)!]]\Pi^x(1 - \Pi)^{(n-x)}$, where n is the number of songs on the album, Π is the probability of any one song being good, and x is the number of good songs.

Chapter 14

1. John Cullen, "Structural Aspects of the Architectural Profession," in Judith Blau, Mark E. La Gory, and John S. Pipkin, eds., *Professionals and Urban Form* (Albany: State University of New York Press, 1983), p. 287.

2. John Worthington, "The Changing Context of Professional Practice," in David Nicol and Simon Pilling, eds., *Changing Architectural Education: Toward a New Professionalism* (New York: Spon Press, 2000), p. 33.

3. Ibid.

4. Jason Timberlake and Stephen Kieran, *Refabricating Architecture: How Manufacturing Methodologies Are Poised to Transform Building Construction* (New York: McGraw Hill, 2004), p. 29.

5. Ray Porter, *The Greatest Benefit to Mankind* (New York: W. W. Norton, 1997), p. 351.

Chapter 16

1. Le Corbusier, *The City of To-morrow and Its Planning* (New York: Dover, 1987), p. 164.

2. Christopher Jarrett, "Social Practice: Design Education and Everyday Life," in David Nicol and Simon Pilling, eds., *Changing Architectural Education: Toward a New Professionalism* (New York: Spon Press, 2000), p. 59.

3. American Institute of Architects, *Architect's Handbook of Professional Practice*, 14th ed. (Hoboken: Wiley 2008), p. 107.

4. Daniel Herman, "High Architecture," in Jeffery Inaba, Rem Koolhaas, Sze Tsung Leong, and Chuihua Judy Chung, *Project on the City 2: Harvard Design School Guide to Shopping* (Cambridge, MA: Taschen, 2001), p. 397.

5. Adam L. Penenberg, "All Eyes on Apple," *Fast Company,* December 2007–January 2008, p. 134.

Chapter 18

1. Bernard Tschumi, "One, Two, Three: Jump," in Martin Pearce and Maggie Toy, eds., *Educating Architects* (London: Academy Editions, 1995), p. 24.

2. Available at http://www.bdonline.co.uk/story.asp?sectioncode=426&storycode=3134153&c=1.

3. James Bailey, "The Case History of Failure," *Architectural Forum* 23, no. 5 (December 1965), p. 22.

4. Rem Koolhaas, "Introduction to the End," in Rem Koolhaas and Bruce Mau, *S, M, L, XL* (New York: Monacelli Press, 1995), p. 1252.

Chapter 19

1. Michael Kimmelman, "The Architect, His Client, Her Husband and a House Named Turbulence," *New York Times Magazine,* May 21, 2006.

2. Colin Stansfield Smith, "A Regressive Approach," in Martin Pearce and Maggie Toy, eds., *Educating Architects* (London: Academy Editions, 1995), p. 40.

Chapter 20

1. Mary McLeod, "Architecture and Politics in the Reagan Era: From Postmodernism to Deconstructivism," *Assemblage* 8 (1989).

2. Samuel Mockbee, "The Role of the Citizen Architect," in Bryan Bell, ed., *Good Deeds, Good Design: Community Service through Architecture* (New York: Princeton Architectural Press, 2004), p. 152.

3. Zaha Hadid, "Another Beginning," in Peter Noever, ed., *The End of Architecture? Documents and Manifestos* (Munich: Prestel, 1993), p. 26.

Chapter 22

1. Daniel Libeskind, *Breaking Ground* (New York: Riverhead Books, 2004), p. 218.

2. John Ruskin, *The Seven Lamps of Architecture* (New York: Dover, 1989), p. 241.

3. Juhanni Pallasmaa, *The Eyes of the Skin: Architecture and the Senses* (West Sussex, UK: Wiley-Academy, 2005), p. 30.

Chapter 24

1. Steven D. Levitt and Stephen J. Dubner, *Freakonomics* (New York: Harper Collins, 2005), p. 106.

2. Alain de Botton, *The Architecture of Happiness* (New York: Pantheon, 2006), p. 17.